To
Avan C. Hardwell Sr.

HEAVEN IS REAL

The True Story of Tony Davis

TDM
VISION
BOOKS
A TONY DAVIS MINISTRIES COMPANY
Tony Davis Ministries

Copyright © 2005 Tony Davis Ministries & Avan C. Hardwell Sr.

All rights reserved. No part of this book may be reproduced in any form or by any electronic or mechanical means, including information storage and retrieval systems, without permission in writing from the publisher, except by a reviewer, who may quote brief passages in a review.

Cover concept by: Herman Martinez
Cover illustration by: Herman Martinez
Hand lettering by: Avan C. Hardwell Sr.

Tony Davis Ministries is a registered trademark of Tony Davis Ministries, Inc.

Tony Davis Ministries, Inc.
11521 Sierra Sky Dr.
Whittier, CA. 90602

Visit our Web sit at
www.tonydavisgospel.com

Originally published in paperback by TDM
First United States Paperback Printing: September 2012

Pastor Ron Roberson

The miracle of Tony Davis is an experience we all can learn from. From the day I met him I knew he would be a friend for life. I will never forget the day I saw him in the Hospital.

As I walked through the corridors of that cold, dreary place, looking at all of the sick and diseased people, a feeling of depression fell over me. I said to my self, "Tony deserves better than this". As I entered his room, I heard people moaning and crying out in pain, but I looked up and saw the joy of Jesus glowing through tubes, monitors, splints, and IV's: it was Tony. Despite the pain and trauma he had suffered from the gunshot wounds, he was still smiling and glowing, which changed my life and renewed my walk with Christ.

Tony's ordeal did more for me than any sermon, song or testimony I have ever heard; it has been a lesson for a lifetime. My job was to accept the lesson, love the person, and put what I have learned to use in all other relationships and areas of my life, and that has been my mission. This wonderful man of God has found forgiveness in his heart for his oppressors and he has turned a potentially depressing situation into a powerful life-changing testimony. Tony has taught me to work as if you do not need the money; love as if you have never been hurt, and to dance as though no one is watching…*Ron Roberson is the host of CNN Headline News "Local Edition" Producer / Director of Miracle Productions..*
Pastor of On Fire Ministries in California

The Honorable Mayor Fred Esco

Through my life's experiences, I have learned if God be for us, who can be against us? The devil comes to kill, steal and destroy, but God gives us abundant life. If we continue to acknowledge God in all of our ways, all things are possible, if we only believe.

Tony, the anointing is upon your life, and the enemy recognizes the strength that God has given you to be His messenger of hope, prosperity, and deliverance. Your life experiences were meant to destroy you, but instead, they helped you to recognize your own strengths and prepared you for the Kingdom of God. Your testimony is exemplary that all things work together for the good of them who love the Lord.

Life has taught me that what God has for me, is for me, and He shall perform the work He began in me. Tony, when your pathway seems dark, look to the Light; look to the hills from whence cometh your help; look to Jesus, the author and finisher of your faith. I pray that God continues to elevate you and enlarge your territory and that you will glorify Him in all things, in all your success. Moreover, I pray that He continues to shield you with the blood of Jesus and that you will recognize that it is grace and mercy that brought you out of the darkness into the marvelous light. The citizens of Canton are proud of you, and we support your mission for Christ. Keep the faith and stay focused on your purpose....

*Mayor Fred Esco (***Mayor of Canton, Mississippi)**

This book is dedicated to the memory of Red

He may have been my stepfather,
and though I always called him Red,

He was definitely my daddy!

And we know that all things work together for the good of them that love God, to them who are called according to his purpose

Contents

A Little Family History…………………………………7

Making Ends Meet……………………………………..24

First Miracle in My Life……………………………….33

The Desire to Sing……………………………………..36

The City of Angels…………………………………….42

Getting My Feet Wet…………………………………..45

The R & T Collections………….……………………..55

A Vision from the Holy Spirit….……………………..78

Georgia………………………….……………………..81

A New Life and a New Wife…………………………..86

A Change of Heart…………………………………….96

The New Me………………………………………….104

My First Gospel Video……………………………….110

The Good Samaritan………………………...………..133

Little Vietnam………………………………………..147

Absent from the Body and Present with the Lord……...158

Resurrected from Death………………………………161

Vengeance Is Mine, Saith the Lord…………………..177

One

" A LITTLE FAMILY HISTORY "

Tony Davis at the age of 3 years old

My name is Tony Davis, and I was born December 5th, 1963 in a small town just north of Jackson, Mississippi, called Canton, which is home to the Grammy Award Winning Gospel Group, The Canton Spirituals. One of the group's members, Cornelius Watkins, was one of my high school classmates.

My mother, Lillie C. Hill, is a short, full-figured woman, who is still quite beautiful in my eyes, though time has taken its toll on her. Her face and hands reveal years of hard work, scrubbing floors, shelling peas, and sewing clothes for white folk just to put food on the table, along with the challenges and stress of raising six children.

I grew up in an average sized family of three boys and

three girls; I was next to the baby boy. Even though my mother and stepfather struggled to keep things together, I remember having a pleasant childhood. Life was good, even though times were, somewhat, hard. In those days, parents did not have to focus too much on keeping their children out of trouble because children had more respect for their elders. Today's generation of kids, do not even begin to come close, when it comes to having respect for their parents or older people, in general.

If a neighbor saw one of us doing something we should not have been doing, they either would whip us themselves or made sure our parents knew what we had done. Most of the time, though, they would just whip us, phone our parents, tell them of our misdeed, and then our parents would whip us, too. Everybody watched out for everyone else's children, including their own.

These days, however, you had better not even consider touching someone else's child, no matter what they have done.

Kids today get away with just about everything under the sun you can think of, and, in my opinion, it does not take a genius to figure out why. The way the laws are set up today, a parent no matter how much they may care about or need to chastise their own child, cannot for fear of legal retaliation, or worst; going to jail.

The Holy Bible plainly says in the book of Proverbs 13:24, "He that spares the rod hates his son: but he that loves him will chasten him diligently."

My mother must have loved me fiercely because she would put a rod to my butt if she merely thought I was thinking about doing something wrong. I thank God for her, and I love her for doing what she had to do every time I

deserved it. Her "tough-love" is what helped to mold me

into the man that I am today.

It literally blew my mind when I learned that a child could sue and obtain a divorce from his or her parents. What kind of society do we live in when children can get a divorce from their parents? In my opinion, it is a society where laws are not in place for the benefit of the young, growing population of children destined to one day be the leaders of our world.

Instead they're designed simply to benefit the sick, morally depraved minds and lifestyles of men and women in high places, whose sole objective in life is to legally get away with their own lascivious and abominable ways of life.

It should be more than obvious, to anyone with half-a-brain, that the lawmakers of our society care absolutely nothing about our children, nor their own. Their only interests are in their own perverted ways of life. I suppose they assume they have nothing to lose and that, by the time children are old enough to take over and destroy the world, they will be long dead and gone, anyway.

So, again, I truly thank God for my mother, and that she wasted no time in giving me a truly righteous butt whipping when I deserved it. Her discipline only showed her undying love and concern for my well-being and future as an adult in a world that saw me as inferior, sub-human, and undeserving of a fair chance from the very beginning, simply because of the color of my skin.

On the other hand, my mother always instilled in me that "God will make a way somehow," and I believed her because I knew that she believed in and loved God.

Mother was and is still a praying woman. When I was a little boy, I would see her on her knees every single night, praying before she went to bed. Sometimes she'd pray for a long, long time, and as she did, I'd stand close to the heater in the hallway trying to keep warm as I watched her pour her heart out before God. Then I would do the same before I went to bed. She was on her knees so much and for so long until one day I asked her if her knees hurt when she prayed. All she said was, "Baby, Jesus' whole body hurt when they nailed him to the cross." Even though I was just a child, I thought her response was deep.

***

That same night I went to my room to pray and stayed on my knees for a long time, just like my mother. After I finished, I jumped in bed and closed my eyes. I don't know about mother's knees, but mine were certainly sore.

As I lay there with my eyes closed, trying to fall asleep, I suddenly felt a strange sensation move over my entire body. It felt as though something wonderful was happening to my spirit; my inner man, whom at the time, I knew nothing about, but I kept lying there with my eyes closed, surrendering to whatever was happening to me.

After a while, I opened my eyes and looked up at the window, located just above my head a little to the right and noticed that the curtains were wide open. I thought that was unusual because the curtains were not usually open, and outside of my window, I could normally hear frogs, crickets, and all kinds of animals and bugs making noises, but that night was different. Everything was so quiet, peaceful, and still. There was no wind blowing or anything. It was weird, but I felt so wonderful and full of peace that I had to share it with someone.

I called out to my younger brother, Leo, who was fast asleep in his bed across from mine. When he did not answer, I called his name again, "Leo!" He still didn't answer. I shouted louder, "Leo," but to no avail. Leo was sound asleep.

I thought about waking mother or my stepfather, Red, but I did not want to leave the room for fear that whatever, or whomever was in the room with me would be gone when I returned with an adult. It was probably all for the best because parents usually chalk up the unexplainable things that children say to their vivid imaginations. Whatever happened in my room that night was not my imagination. It was as real as life itself.

I did not know what was happening to me. I just knew that it was something good. I believe with everything in my heart that God was in the room with me that night. I had no doubt that it was Him because I had been told about this kind of thing many times before by my step-grandmother, Callie Davis, who would always be jumping around in church as though her clothes had been set on fire. She would be shouting at the top of her lungs, thanking the Holy Spirit for being her friend and comforter in a time of need. She was on fire all right. She was on fire with the presence of the Holy Spirit flowing through her entire being.

Now, He had come into my room to let me know that He was my friend, too. I was in total awe.

But having no one to share this glorious experience with, I found myself just lying there in bed with my hands clasped tightly together in a position of prayer; praising and thanking God for coming to see me.

Though it might sound strange or even a little unbelievable, I truly believe that on that night the Holy Spirit placed a strong desire in my heart to seek out my purpose in life. A desire that has strengthened and ultimately led me to Christ, and kept me from going through so many of life's most disastrous, and discouraging obstacles.

To this very day there are times that I don't feel like

getting on my knees to pray, but during those times, I think about what my mother said after I asked her if it hurt her knees to pray for so long. Her simple, but extremely powerful, reply makes getting on my knees so much easier.

My stepfather's name was Odis Hill, but as far back as I can remember, Leo and I always called him Red.

Everyone else called him "Mr. Hill" or "Big Red" because he was a big, light-skinned black man, who did not take any mess from anyone.

Red's, mother's name was Maggie Hill. Maggie was a skinny, tall, black woman who married a short, skinny, white man named Champ Hill. They lived in another small, Mississippi town where Red was born, and grew up, called Rakin County Mississippi. Back in those days, in Mississippi, white men would hang a black man for even looking at a white woman, let alone marrying one.

Somehow, Red's parents were able to stay together, even though they were probably taunted and given a hard time by whites during a time and era when hate, prejudice, and injustice against blacks and, for that matter, anyone who cared for them, was blatantly made known. I guess that is why Red's temper was so short; like the fuse at the end of a firecracker.

Nevertheless, for as short as Red's temper could be, he had a heart that was as gentle as a Lamb's. He cursed an awful lot but, regardless of his way of life which wasn't always lived by the "Good Book", he always made sure that we lived in a nice home, had plenty of food on the table and, no matter how bad things became, he never let our lights get turned off.

My mother's, father's name was Anderson Davis, but most people knew him as Sonny. He was a huge, dark-skinned, black man who always wore overalls. To be an uneducated black man, grandfather had a good job working for the Illinois Central Railroad Company for many years. He would sometimes come by our house to pick me up when I was no more than four years old and give me a ride in the back of his truck after church on Sundays. I loved when he did that, and I think that is why he was so faithful in doing it. Mother said he loved his family and every chance he got he did all that he could to see that they were happy.

My grandmother, Fannie Sanders Johnson, was mixed with Indian and had long, beautiful black hair. As she got older, I noticed that her hair only turned gray at the root. I thought that was a little strange, so I asked her one-day if she dyed her hair. She told me "no" and that for some strange reason, her mother's hair did the same thing. My grandmother died in May of 1997.

Mother told me that my grandmother had an older brother named Tampa who, like Red, did not take any mess from white folk, either. Mother said that Tampa looked like a white man. All of his features, including his hair made him look white, even though he was black. She said he always stood up for his rights, no matter what. One day, the Ku Klux Klan killed Uncle Tampa because of his outspokenness. He was so concerned, I suppose, about being just as respected as any white man, that he just did not know when it was best not to say anything.

After the KKK killed Uncle Tampa, they placed his body on the railroad tracks so that a train could run over him to make it look like an accident. I was told his body was severed and torn so badly until his remains had to be picked up with a shovel. My grandmother was deeply, affected by his death.

Mother told me that before Uncle Tampa was killed, he told my grandmother "If anything ever happens to me, be sure to go to the plum bushes, close to the railroad tracks, and dig up a bucket full of money that I have buried behind the tree." My grandmother never went back in search of the money because she was afraid of what the KKK would have done to her had they found out. For all anybody knows, that bucket of money is still there.

It was obvious to me from a very young age that the world in which I suddenly found myself a part of was not quite right.

There was something mournfully wrong with the way people treated each other, and there was, particularly, something wrong with the way that whites treated men and women of color.

I grew up in a segregated neighborhood, which, needless to say, I hated profoundly. As a child, I hated and despised the white population because of the inarguable suffering they devotedly and joyously inflicted on the black race, which to me made absolutely no sense at all.

We were hated so much, and thought of as being so low and sub-human, that all living conditions and activities that would cause blacks to come into contact with whites were segregated: the drinking fountains, restaurants, and even public bathrooms.

A white man would rather let a stray dog drink from the same fountain from which he drank rather than let a black man, woman, or child put their lips anywhere near it.

It was unbelievable. I could not understand how almost an entire race of people could be so inherently perverted, both emotionally and spiritually. White people were so praetorian in mind, heart, and spirit until they truly believed themselves to be completely superior and dissimilar from everyone else on earth; so much so, until they absolutely found no pleasure in doing anything short of torturing, raping, debasing, and ultimately murdering every man, woman, and child of color.

And they lived in these huge, beautiful white homes on one side of the railroad tracks while we, even though we were blessed as were many of our family and neighbors, lived in houses that were hardly comparable to the other side of the tracks. It really didn't bother me as much as a child because I really did not understand what was going on. I just knew that something was not right.

Besides, I had too much fun playing in our back yard, up and down the streets or over a friend's house to be worried about too much of anything else.

It was not until I began to grow up and the realization that things were different, because of the color of my skin that those feelings of hate, despise, and anger came into play.

There was one white woman, however, whom I found to be nice. Her name was Mrs. Carolyn. She would pick mother up early every morning to baby-sit, clean, and sew clothes and drapes for her.

There were many times when mother would come home and say, "Good Lord, those white folks nearly worked me to death today!" She would then sit down for a few minutes to try to catch her breath, but before she ever really did, she would be up and in the kitchen cooking dinner.

Aside from Mrs. Carolyn, I really hated whites in those days, and for years, I used to pray and ask God why He allowed white people to inflict so much pain and torment on black people.

After a while, I even began to believe that God hated the black race as much as white people did because He allowed them to do everything to us that came into their minds. It was not until many, many years later that I reconsidered my feelings concerning the white race as a whole. Thank God for the renewing of the mind, which comes with the gift of salvation.

Since I have been, saved, though, I have met and become very good friends with a white woman named Korolla who lives in Los Angeles and has proven to be one of the best friends I could have ever hoped to have. We have been friends now for some fourteen years, and I realize today that in God's eyes there is no color line, just the heart of each individual person.

The Bible says in Romans 2:11, "For there is no respect of person with God," which simply means that God does not show favoritism to anyone.

Mamma' Lillie C & Tony   Mamma' & Red (Odis Hill)

Red, WWI   Grandma Fannie Johnson

Step-grandmother Callie Davis   Granddaddy Anderson & Family

Tony and Leo playing Gun Smoke

Leo, Dee-Dee, Maurice, & Tony at 10 years old

Vera, Robert Lee, Vickie, Charlie Mae, Tony, & Leo

Karolle D'Maggio

Two

" MAKING ENDS MEET "

Making a living was somewhat hard back in those days for blacks, but Red had many hustles that he did just to make ends meet and to put food on the table. Some of his hustles were fun, in the fact that it benefited Leo and me in more ways than food, clothing, and shelter. Like the time he worked for a small, taxicab company driving a big, old station wagon. He would drive Leo, me, and a few kids from the neighborhood to and from school everyday. He would always seat Leo and I on the front seat next to him, close to the heater, just to make sure that we were warm. That was fun.

Some of Red's other hustles were not so fun, though, like gambling. Red was definitely a gambling man and would stay out late every Friday and Saturday night, sometimes as late as one or two o'clock in the morning.

On Sunday mornings, he would give Leo and me one or two bucks each to go to church with, but we would only put a dime into the offering basket. If Leo and I felt extremely generous, though, we would put in as much as a whopping quarter, and then save the rest to buy ice cream, cotton candy, and peanuts during the week on the way home from school.

There were other times when Red would come home late at night with his lip bleeding and his stomach aching from beatings exacted by the local, white policemen, who would also take the money, he won from gambling. He told me the police would sometimes watch and wait like wolves in the night to see who'd win a gambling game, and then follow them as they drove home or wherever they were going, hoping for a chance to rob and beat them up.

Back in those days on the pitch black, wooded roads of Mississippi, it was easy for the police to take advantage of black people. Red told me they followed and beat him up on many occasions late at night on his way home after winning.

When I think about it now, I know that God was always watching over Red, even as he gambled. I believe God knew that Red figured he had to gamble to support his family because he knew of no other way to do it. In fact, I know God was looking out for him because Red said to me once that sometimes some of the people that the police followed never arrived home, and were never seen or heard from again. His words were, "That's just the price we sometimes pay to feed our families."

Another way mother and Red made ends meet was through garage sales that white folks had. Actually, it did not matter if money was tight or not, mother simply loved shopping at those garage sales. She and her girlfriend, Mrs. Hattie, practically lived at them.

Sometimes when Ms. Hattie did not feel like driving, Red would have to drive because mother had never learned how. She would even take Leo and me with them, but my sisters and older brother never came along. They were too ashamed and afraid that their friends might see them. We would have to wear those old rummage sale clothes, too.

Sometimes I hated that, but not as much as Leo did. He would just refuse to put them on.

He would give mother one hard time if she even

tried to make him put on those old clothes, that is until Red got wind of it.

When Red spoke, Leo would waste no time putting them on, but he would still have a big frown on his face.

Mother even told me about a job she once had at the Canton Poultry Market, a local, chicken-processing plant. She would get up every morning by five to be at work by six for a measly twelve dollars a week.

Twelve dollars, for an entire week's worth of hard, labor! I could not believe it! That was nothing but chicken feed; no pun intended. Sometimes mother did not get off work until ten at night, depending on whatever time the truck arrived with chickens that had to be slaughtered. Even though the cost of living was far less in those days, I still consider that rate of pay nothing but slave wages. Again, no pun intended. In all honesty, I have a problem if someone tries to pay me as little as thirteen or fourteen dollars an hour.

Mother also worked many odd jobs. She is a very talented and gifted woman. She could sew so well that she even made drapes for the town's court and jail house, just by going down to the buildings, looking at what they wanted her to do, and then without taking any type of measurements, go home and make them. Believe me, the drapes always fit perfectly.

She was also an interior decorator. She could walk into a room and visualize just the right accents, types of furniture, flowers, and the most beautiful pictures imaginable to hang on the walls, and bring forth any room's beauty. When she was finished, the whole room would be perfect and beautifully decorated.

Believe me, I am not being biased, merely

because she is my mother. The fact is she is just good at those types of things. When I think about it all now I feel, somewhat saddened for my mother because she spent most of her time designing rooms and making clothes for others. She never really got a chance to use her talents for her own success, but she did make our home a beautiful, warm, and very comfortable place to live.

She made some of our clothes, too. Once, when I was in the junior high school band, I wanted a new suit for the school's Christmas musical, but Mother did not have the money to purchase a suit, so she went to a bedroom window and took down the curtains.

A few days later, I had a shiny new, red, satin suit that she had fashioned from the curtains, and it was one of the finest suits I have ever had.

It was funny, though, because everybody in school thought I paid a lot of money for that suit. When the other kids complimented me on the suit and tried to guess how much it cost, I just laughed because I knew that it was just a pair of old bedroom curtains that used to flap at the window during a good breeze.

I have learned many good things from my mother, all of which have become a part of who I am. Whenever mother did things for other people, she did it entirely from the bottom of her heart and never looked for anything in return. That is just the kind of woman she was, and still is today. I admire her for that, and I can honestly say that same good and wholesome spirit has been passed on to me.

She would always tell all of her children, "Do unto others like you would want them to do unto you," or, "When folk do you wrong, two wrongs don't make it right, so just treat them kindly with a smile and keep your head up, no matter what."

Mom and Red were strict on us, too, and I realize now that it was only because they loved us and wanted us to grow into the finest adults that we could possibly be.

When it came to our bedtimes, they were even stricter about that, but mother would allow me to stay up late with her, most of the times, watching her sew as I laid against her. I would snuggle close to her so that we could talk, while she sewed. We would talk about everything under the sun, sometimes until three o'clock in the morning. That's when Red usually got home from work or whatever hustle he had going on, and then she would stop, put away everything so that Red could go to bed and get some rest, and then she'd finally make me go to bed, too.

The best part I can remember about growing up was when mother woke us up early every morning for a good, old-fashioned, home-cooked breakfast.

Sometimes she didn't even have to wake us because the smell of eggs and sausage frying, biscuits baking, and grits simmering in an old pot had an aroma so strong that it would flow through the entire house, picking on everybody's nose. The aroma was so incredible and full of flavor that there was no way we could have continued to sleep, even if we wanted to. One of our favorite treats, were her T-cakes. I would sit in the kitchen, next to the cookie jar, and eat as many as

I could. Boy, those were truly the best of days.

So, I guess I can say, despite the hard times my family often had to endure when I was growing up, and, believe me, we did have our share, when I sum it all up, things could have been a lot worse. Therefore, I think I can honestly say I had a decent childhood.

My Shiny Red Suit

The Dinner Table

Three

" First Miracle In My Life "

The first time God revealed His awesome power in my life was when He healed me from a severe sickness that was weakening the bone in my left leg. I was in the sixth grade and I, somehow, developed a disease that caused me to fall down every time I would stand up and try to walk.

As I think about it now, I know that even then, Satan was trying to destroy my life or lame my body so that I could not do the work that God had planned for me to do from the very foundation of this world.

Satan knows when God has a special calling on a person's life, even when you are just a child, or unborn and helpless in your mother's womb. He is willing and desires to do all he can within his evil, perverted power, including taking your life, if God allows it, just to interfere with God's plans for you.

He is truly cruel and seeks specifically to kill, steal, and destroy all human life. This means that we must always; above all things remember that he has nothing to lose. He knows that he can never, under any circumstances imaginable, return to the position of favor and grace that he once had in God. He knows that his soul is condemned to an eternity in Hell and that there is no forgiveness for him.

You may think that I am crazy to say this, but I truly believe in my heart that if Satan had the opportunity to repent to God for having the audacity to conceive the thought of building a kingdom that would rise above God's, he would fall down on his knees this very moment and beg for forgiveness. However, he cannot find forgiveness with God, and he knows that God will not and cannot lie, no matter what. For this reason Satan is very angry.

In fact, Satan is stark raving mad! Mad at every living creature on the face of this planet, and he is out to kill every man, woman, and child that he can get his hands on.

The disease in my leg worsened to the point that the doctors told my mother there was nothing else that they could do for me, except amputate.

"The Lord is going to heal Tony's leg," she told the doctors, "so don't worry about cutting it off."

I imagine the doctors had not one single ounce of faith in what my mother was saying and probably thought she was crazy, and uttered under their breath, "Sure, Lady...whatever you say."

They made an appointment for me to return to their office the following week. Well, we did, and sure enough, after the doctor examined me, he found that my leg had healed completely. The doctors could not believe it and wanted to send me to a lab in Jackson to have more tests run.

"No. There's no need to do that," mother said, "The Lord has done His work."

That is just the kind of faith she had in God then, and still has in Him today. She believed that God would, could, and was willing to do everything within His will for those who love and serve Him with all their heart. I also believed that.

Four

" THE DESIRE TO SING "

My desire to sing began in a Baptist church when I first heard my Aunt Callie Mae sing Amazing Grace. It was there, sitting beside my mother one hot, Sunday morning that I knew singing was what I wanted to do. When I say it was hot, believe me, it was hot! Back then our church couldn't afford one of those fancy, electric fans, but what we did have plenty of were those paper fans that you hold in your hand; compliments from your local funeral home.

Every member in church, including the pastor, was fanning like crazy, trying to cool off from the searing heat. We were all sweating hard, and the heat was putting me to sleep.

As I was dozing off, I remember seeing the pastor as he rose to his feet, made his way to the altar, and then looked out into the congregation with a smile.

"Candidates for baptism, Christian experience, or joinin' a new church home?" he asked the congregation, waited a few moments for someone to respond, and then turned and faced the choir.

"While ya'll make up ya' minds on how ya comin' to the Lord, I'm gon' ask sista' Callie Mae to bless us with that beautiful voice the Lord done gave her and sing somethin' for us."

Everybody started clapping and cheering as the pastor walked back to his chair. They were excited that Aunt Callie was about to sing. By the time the pastor sat down, two deacons had just finished setting a couple of chairs in front of the pulpit for those who wanted to come to the altar and find salvation from their sins.

Suddenly, Aunt Callie began to sing. She hit a couple of notes of Amazing Grace accappella-style as the piano player, a huge, full-figured woman named Ms. Morgan, who was Holy Ghost-filled and could sing like God knows what, herself, pecked out a couple of keys on the piano. Within seconds, Ms. Morgan joined in with Aunt Callie, and off they went.

It was the most amazing thing that I had ever seen and heard in my life. Aunt Callie's voice was beautiful! I had never heard anyone sing like that before and I was captivated. She sounded better than anyone I had heard over the radio, and I knew, from the very first moment she opened her mouth and began to sing, that that was what I wanted to do. From then on, whenever I came to church I got a front row seat and stared into Aunt Callie's mouth, trying to figure out how she sang that way, and so good.

I thought to myself, "Is something in her mouth making her sound so good?"

It just had to be! How could anybody sing like that? I was determined to find out what was in her throat because nobody sounded like that.

After I turned sixteen, I joined the choir. I was too afraid to sing solo until Ms. Morgan called on me one day during rehearsal, because mother had told her that I could play trumpet and organ really well. I could play the trumpet all right, but the organ, not quite as well. I could only play by looking at numbers from an organ book. To this day, I do not know what playing the trumpet had to do with singing, but that was how it all started. Still, though, mother thought I was one of the best.

When Ms. Morgan called me up front to sing a solo I thought I was going to fall out.

Mother said, "Don't be afraid to use what the Lord has given you."

Therefore, I made a valiant attempt, and for the most part, it turned out quite good. Two weeks later, mother said, "The devil is busy. You need to get closer to Jesus by letting him into your heart." "I already did," I replied.

She looked at me for a moment, and then smiled.

"Good," she said, "then go sit on the morning bench so that you can be baptized."

I did as she told me, with no questions asked, and Leo was right behind me, as always.

From that point on, all the way through high school, I remained a part of the church choir, but I still did not think I was good enough to sing in front of an audience, so I just sang background.

My thing was playing the trumpet. I was thrilled when I made the high school band because they had the best band uniforms around, and they could play, too.

After graduation, I really did not know which way to go with my life. I just believed that life would be good as long as I kept the Lord first.

About a year later, I moved to Orlando, Florida to stay with my aunt Hattie McCree, who was the best aunt that anyone could have. She and my cousins treated me really well, and they did all they could to make me feel right at home.

Aunt Hattie and I went to church almost every Sunday, unfortunately, though, something was still missing in my life, and I had a strong desire to find out what it was. I felt like I needed to be doing something to help people and to let them know that God loved them.

Auntie Callie Mae & Family

Cousin Patricia & Family who live in Florida

Five

" THE CITY OF ANGELS "

Something was continuously pulling and tugging at my spirit, drawing me to Los Angeles. I had never been there before, but I had to find out what that something was.

Two years later, after much prayer and seeking God, I finally made the move to the "Land of La-La." When I got there I hardly knew what to expect or what I was looking for, but I knew that I would know what it was as soon as I found it.

I lived with a friend from home, sleeping on his living room sofa, and then soon landed a job working at the Day's Inn Hotel, close to the airport, driving a shuttle bus.

Things were going all right and I had been in Los Angeles for just a little more than a year, when I received a phone call on my job telling me that Red had died.

I had no idea what I was going to do about getting home. I had not yet saved enough money to catch an airplane.

After I hung up the telephone, I went back to work and began praying to God, asking him to make a way for me to go home, and, not to my amazement, it was not long before He answered my prayers. My co-workers had all gotten together and took up a collection of money, and then gave it to me to make the trip home by bus.

When I finally arrived home, everyone was trying to be strong and encouraging one another because Red never liked to see anyone cry, particularly, grown men.

At the funeral home, and while in the company of Leo and my older brother, Robert Lee, I thought I could take it until I looked into the casket and saw Red lying there so still, and silent. My heart felt like it was literally bleeding. It hurt to see such a strong man like Red lying so motionless: never to get up again.

That was one of the most difficult moments of my life because I remember one day Red and I sat on the front porch and he said, "Tony, one day I'm going to leave this world. Always be a man and do what is right.

"Now, twenty years later, I still think about Red, who never showed love by hugging or pampering, yet he showed it in his own way by making sure everyone was happy.

I am immensely grateful for everything that he ever taught me. He may have been my stepfather, and though I always called him Red, he was definitely my daddy. I am blessed more than I can express, and a better man because of Red's presence in my life.

A few months after my father's death, once I was back in Los Angeles, I enrolled into a business college located in Hollywood and took up accounting.

When I graduated, I remember sitting in my chair throughout the whole ceremony thinking to myself, "Wow, I wish Red were here to see me now. He would have been so proud."

Six

" Getting My Feet Wet "

One day at school, I was sitting in the lunchroom eating with some friends, when suddenly, one of the other students began singing a song I had heard over the radio called Wild Flower by "New Birth". It was one of my favorite songs and this brother sounded great singing it.

The only other person that I had ever heard that could sing that well was my Aunt Callie.

As I sat there, listening in awe as the brother sang his heart out, I found it hard to believe that the male voice could sound so touching. It created a completely new desire in me to sing. I wanted to sound like him, but only better. Everyone stopped what he or she was doing, just to listen to him sing. He was great!

After he finished singing, everyone in the lunchroom immediately began clapping and cheering.

As they did, I went over and introduced myself to him. He shook my hand and said that his name was Jeff Fincher, and that he was from Gary, Indiana. I told him that I was looking to join a group and asked him if he needed a background singer.

"Sure," he exclaimed.

We hooked up and immediately began rehearsing over the weekends. A few weeks later, another singer named Stephen Brooks joined our group. Stephen's mother was one of the original singers for a famous female R & B singing group from the sixties called "The Shirelles."

We called ourselves J. T. S., which is of course the acronym for Jeff, Tony, and Stephen.

During the next three years, we sang a lot in places like The Roxy, Club Vertigo, Carlos & Charlie's, and The Speak Easy. At the time, these were some of Hollywood's hottest nightspots. We were also performing at many other clubs in Southern California and were becoming quite popular.

We opened for acts like Bobby Brown and performed on the Arsenio Hall Show during his first season. We were even the star attraction on a musical showcase sponsored by actor Isabel Sanford, a.k.a. "Weezy" of the famed television series "The Jefferson's." The list goes on-and-on, and, if I must say so myself, we were good!

One day, following one of our shows, I told Jeff that I wanted to sing lead, sometimes.

"Your voice isn't ready to sing lead yet," he said.

"Well, when do you think my voice will be ready?" I politely asked.

He looked at me, sort of rolled his eyes, and said, "I'll let you know."

Well, after that conversation I knew that Jeff would do everything he could to keep me in the background, at least for as long as I allowed him to.

A few weeks later, Stephen went out on tour, overseas, with his mother, and "J.T.S." became "Jeff & Tony". We started doing a few new songs with me leading small parts, but as far as Jeff was concerned, I was still his background singer.

Shortly after that, I figured it was time for me to branch out on my own, but I did not quite know which way to go. Then, one Wednesday night, when I went with a friend, Tony Novel, to sing at a small, cozy little spot called, "Bolero," I found out.

Bolero was a cool spot, a beginner's joint. You could sing, recite poetry, or even play an instrument, if you had the nerve.

Tony Novel quickly jumped on stage and sang two songs. He sounded great! After he finished, he looked out at me. I never thought for a moment that he was about to call on me, but he did.

"Ladies and gentleman!" he yelled, "I'd like to introduce to you another great singer! His name is Tony Davis, and I would like him to come up and sing something. It'll be his first time out on his own, so be kind." I could not believe my ears. He actually singled me out. Everybody in the club started cheering and clapping. My bottom lip dropped and felt as though it had landed on the floor! I was in total shock! I had only sung background for Jeff.

I knew that I wanted to sing lead, but I thought I would get to choose the time and place when it would happen. Tony Novel, however, had proven me wrong.

Suddenly, everything around me began moving in slow motion and, even though the club boasted a full house that night, it seemed as though I was suddenly alone, surrounded by all of these people, who kept clapping, cheering, and staring at me, waiting for me to get up and sing a song.

I wanted to back out, but I could not. It was what I had been waiting for! This was what I had desired so strongly to do with my life every since the first time I heard Aunt Callie sing Amazing Grace that day in church.

As I rose to my feet, my heart began racing, faster, and faster. The closer I got to the stage, the harder my heart pounded. It was beating so hard; I thought it was going to jump out of my chest. Until that moment, I had never been so afraid in my life. The more I thought about getting on that stage, singing, in front of all those people, the stronger the vile and bitter taste of fear grew on the back of my tongue, staining it like the horrid taste of a tablespoon of cod-liver oil.

Finally, I began walking toward the stage, and though it was only a few feet away, it felt like the longest walk in the world.

Finally, after what seemed like an eternity, I arrived on stage and stood next to Tony Novel.

He whispered in my ear, "You've got a nice voice, man! Go ahead! You can do it! It's time for you to stop singing background for Jeff and do your own thing."

I looked at Tony Novel for a moment, wondering if I could really sing solo in front of an audience, even though it was what I had wanted to do all along, and then I reluctantly took the microphone from his hand and looked out into the audience.

Every eye in the house was on me. Even though they were supportive, clapping and cheering me on, I thought I was going to die!

Another few seconds' passed as I pondered what I was going to sing, and then suddenly began singing, Always and Forever, a hit song by Heatwave, one of the 70's hottest singing groups. There will never be another time like the seventies. The sixties, seventies, and eighties boasted nothing but musical geniuses.

Those three decades, in my opinion, produced the greatest songwriters and singers the secular world had ever known. The music of the seventies was so rich then artists today, especially Rap artists, are still sampling anything they can find.

Just before my song ended, I was, without question, surprised that I had brought the house to their feet. They were actually clapping and cheering for me. Not like before when I had first gotten on stage and no one really knew if I was good or not, but because they actually liked what they heard. It was the greatest feeling in the world! As crazy as it may seem, I felt as though I was doing something for the very first time in my life to help people.

They actually liked my performance and it was unbelievable. I felt as though God had given me the voice of song, and with it, I would sing to the world and help them make it through the day. I knew that my singing would bring a smile to someone's face. I had finally found that special something in life.

Graduation, United College of Business
(Thinking, I wish Red could see me!)

Stephen, Jeff, and Tony at the Speakeasy in Hollywood, CA

Tony & Jeff at Saints Elmo Village in Los Angeles

Tony Novell & girlfriend in Japan

Tony & Jeff

Seven

" THE R & T COLLECTIONS "

In the summer of 1990, Jeff and I visited a producer's home named Fred, who had written a few songs and wanted to put together a demo for us. Fred also introduced us to another producer named Reggie Morris, who was also a writer, arranger, keyboard player, and vocalist. The brother was bad! He was also quick on noticing people's ego trips.

After he got a load of Jeff's difficult attitude, he pulled me aside and asked me to give him a call.

"Say, brother, I'm new in town and I'm looking for somebody to work with. I definitely wouldn't mind working with you. You seem like a pretty nice dude," he said.

"Yeah, man...great," I zealously replied.

The next thing I knew we were in the studio for the next six months working on some material we had written. Boy, was I glad! I felt like I was finally making some progress and doing something worthwhile. We called our project, "The R & T Collection."

Soon after we finished all of the recordings, we met another guy named John Parham, who tried to set us up with a record deal, but nothing ever materialized.

I must admit, though, that not getting that record deal was somewhat disheartening, especially after all of the hard work we had put into the songs. We literally poured our very souls into every track that we recorded, while dreaming about making the big time, but those dreams were soon, dashed. Even though we did not get the record deal, I still kept faith in my dreams, and moved forward at full throttle.

That following Saturday evening, Reggie called. He needed me to sing background on some tracks that he was working on with his friend, David Robinson.

On that particular day, it was very hot, and, when I arrived, Reggie and David were exhausted from the heat, but were determined to finish the song.

After Reggie introduced me to David, we immediately went to work. David was dark skinned, about 5'8, and weighed about one hundred and fifty pounds. He had a pleasant speaking voice, a wonderful attitude, and he always greeted everyone with a warm, smile.

His singing voice was nice, too; much better than Jeff's, and it reminded me of the late, Donnie Hathaway, my favorite singer of all time.

David's style of dress was kind of Hollywood, with loud colors, but he was still quite in fashion, especially for that day and time. As I think back on it all, I cannot help laughing, because he had a fake, leopard skin outfit that he loved to wear. He used to front as though he really had it going on. Of course, we all faked like that because we wanted to be the next big superstars; or at least we wanted to look the part, if nothing else, but neither one of us had a dime to our names.

Some of the other brothers we knew, used to dance on Soul Train, which was a popular, dance show that first aired on television back in the early seventies, and still airs today. These cats would be dressed to the tee, just like movie stars, but did not have one red cent, and had to sleep in their cars and wear the same outfit, show-after-show. Talk about putting on airs. After rehearsal was over, David and I exchanged telephone numbers.

"Hey, check it out," he said, "I go to a lot of studios to do auditions. You know, a young brother's tryin' to get a record deal."

"Yeah, I know what you mean," I said.

"The next time I go, if you want, I can give you a buzz and you can tag along. You've got a pretty nice voice, maybe you can get an audition."

"Yeah, that sounds cool," I replied, somewhat excited.

"I also know about a few guys in the Valley that are looking for a couple of singers. We can audition for that, too," he said.

"Okay, that sounds cool" I replied.

Even though I had been in Los Angeles for a couple of years, I didn't know that you could go to different studios to audition for a gig, or how you even got that kind of hook up, but David and I were thinking along the same line, in regard to landing a record deal.

I figured that if he could get a deal and I was on some of the material, it would be almost as good as me getting a deal, too. Even if it was just singing background, at least my voice could be heard on a professional recording, which was better than nothing, and I could start from there.

David and I hit it off quite well, almost immediately, and it was not long before we were hanging out with one another, hopping from club to club. I had a red, T-top, 300ZX with some fat sounds and soft, brown, cream leather interior. The radio was nothing more than a factory installed system, but it sounded good and the ladies loved it. When they saw my car, they lost their minds, and, believe me when I say that I took complete advantage of it. I was picking up women all over town!

Though it sounds crazy, women wanted to sleep with me just for a ride in my car.

At that time, HIV had not surfaced, and had not yet run rampant and there was and still is, for all intent and purposes, very little known about the disease. All I can say today is, I thank God that I did not catch it. It was definitely not because I stayed clear of casual sex that I did not become infected, but by the grace of God.

By then, I had gotten my "Mack" down with the ladies. My voice was getting tight, sounding pretty good, and David and I were dating ladies all over Los Angeles, and, yes, we were having lots of sinful fun.

That's right, I said it. We were having a gang of fun, and anyone that says sin is not fun is simply lying through their teeth. In fact, sin is a ball of fun, and a first class ticket to the fiery pits of hell.

Sin is fun because it is a part of every ones natural, fleshly nature. We are born into sin from the very beginning. You're probably wondering; "how is that possible?" We were all just innocent children when we were born, and knew absolutely nothing about right or wrong."

You may also be thinking, "Nobody just starts lying or stealing all by themselves; it is something that we must be taught to do. Things like that just don't come natural," but they do. Sin is inherent, beginning with the fall of Adam, the first man that God created in His own likeness, and the first man to fall from God's grace. Because of his sin, Adam's punishment has been passed down from generation to generation. The pleasure of sin is what our flesh desires. We must understand that it is our spirit nature, and not our fleshly nature that desires to do the perfect will of God.

Jesus said in the latter verse of Matthew 26:41 that, "The spirit indeed is willing, but the flesh is weak." This simply means that the spirit is willing and desires to do the right thing, but the flesh, the earthly body that our spirit resides in, literally has a mind of its own and is constantly at war against the spirit.

Paul wrote in the book of Galatians 5:16-17, "This I say then, Walk in the Spirit, and ye shall not fulfill the lust of the flesh. For the flesh lusteth against the Spirit, and the Spirit against the flesh: and these are contrary the one to the other: so that ye cannot do the things that ye would."

In this particular scripture, Paul is encouraging everyone to live by the spirit, which wants and desires to do the perfect, will of God. He is saying and instructing us to follow the unction of the spirit, to do the right things, instead of giving in to the constant, lustful wants and desires of the flesh, which always desires to do everything against the will of God. Both the spirit and flesh are in constant war with one another.

They are fighting every single moment of the day and night, even while we sleep, to win the war of wills over our bodies. It is entirely up to every one of us, however, the ultimate rulers of our own lives and bodies to make the right decisions and do the right things in life.

The lure of beautiful women, drugs, money, cars, alcohol, and luxurious living is one heck of a weapon that Satan uses to trap his victims. However, by the grace of God, we have a way to deal with every trap, trick, and deceitful lie that Satan can come up with, and that is through the Holy Spirit of God, sent to us by Jesus Himself as a comforter, and a help in and out of trials and tribulations.

The Apostle John wrote in St. John, chapter 14:26 "But the Comforter, which is the Holy Ghost, whom the Father will send in my name, he shall teach you all things, and bring all things to your remembrance, whatsoever I have said unto you."

Jesus knew by first-hand experience that we, you and I, mere mortals born with a natural, sinful nature, could not fight this spiritual war without spiritual powers to overcome the lusts of the flesh. He understood, and understands today every feeling and desire of the flesh than we could possibly imagine.

Some of you may say something like, "Of course He knows and understands. He is God. He knows everything."

This is only somewhat true, and I say somewhat because the one thing that God could not understand is why we are so easily tempted by the desires of the flesh. God is spirit, but thank God for Jesus.

Hebrews 4:15-16 says "For we have not a high

priest which cannot be touched with the feeling of our infirmities; but was in all points tempted like as we are, yet without sin. Let us therefore come boldly unto the throne of grace, that we may obtain mercy, and find grace to help in time of need."

With God, all things are possible, if you would only repent and believe. This is coming from me, a person who once led a sinful lifestyle of drinking, fornicating with women, and smoking marijuana.

When I fully realized the errors of my ways and decided to repent, I prayed to God for deliverance, and He met me just where I was. He delivered me from that sinful, lost lifestyle, for He knew that I was truly repentant and sorry for the sins I had committed in my life. It was hard, but I had made up my mind to deny my flesh from anything that was contrary to the word of God.

The reason I speak so boldly about sin is because I can truly attest to the fact that God can and will transform any ones lifestyle that is contrary to His will. Sins are sins, no matter what kind of sins they are, and no matter who, where, why, or how they are committed. There is no big sin or little sin In God's eyes. He cannot stand any type of sin or the presents of it.

The purpose of me talking about my sin is to parallel my past lifestyle of drinking, smoking marijuana and fornicating with women, with that of men and women who are for one reason or another trapped in homosexual or lesbian relationship. No matter who you are, or how you live, that type of lifestyle is against the will and word of God, but the good news is that He can and will deliver any one that wishes Him to. Please do not misunderstand me, I am not pointing my finger at anyone because we all have fallen short in one way or another, but rather, to testify that God can transform any lifestyle, just as He transformed the life of the Apostle Paul when he was on his way to Damascus to persecute Christians.

Jesus understands everything that we could possibly feel. He understands our pain and misfortunes, and is therefore compassionate, regarding them. He is our lawyer, our advocate who stands before God, pleading our case because He understands. He understands because He was tempted at all points, which means all situations. The way he lived His life was our example. Remember, He was tempted at all points, but was without sin. He did not yield to the desires of the flesh, and we do not have to, either.

If we are not careful, and take care to listen to that still, faint voice of the Holy Spirit, which will always, urge us to do the right thing, we will fall into Satan's trap, and ultimately into a pit of darkness. We will become none other than the walking dead. However, this will not happen before God has turned us over to a reprobate mind, and that will not happen until He is tired of our life style. This is the worst position any man or woman can be in with God. A reprobate mind is a mind that God has turned over to its own lascivious desires. It only happens to those that God has urged for years, and years, and years to come out from a sinful way of life, but they refuse to do so and continue sinning.

Ultimately, and I stress, if after many years of God's grace upon the lives of sinners, and His beseeching to no avail for them to come out of their sin and seek His face for forgiveness, He will turn them over to that evil thing that they have desired so strongly to do within their hearts. It is at that point that Satan steps back, laughing, and scoffing. He knows at this point, that the chances of them turning their lives over to God for His unbridled, love, care, and understanding are slim-to-none, and the prince of darkness has all but sealed a winning victory in the battle for their soul.

As I said earlier, David and I hit it off right from the start. He was also a womanizer, and always had a different woman on his arm. Every month he had a different girl. Of course, I was no different. I loved women, too, and the more the merrier.

I even dated an older woman, who purchased expensive suits for me in exchange for sexual favors. I had a system that all my friends knew about. If any of them dropped by my pad and the red light was on, they knew not to knock on my door, as I was not about to answer because I was taking care of business. Yet, as I think about it all now, I was no different from a hooker. I was a male whore. Actually, I was a whoremonger and a whore. I provided sexual favors for nice suits, and freebies to young cuties.

Yes, I was the man all right or, at least, I thought I was. David and I were hitting the clubs hard, one right after the other, smoking weed, drinking, you name it. Bartles & James, Gin and Juice, and Kahlua and cream were my poisons, and if I remember correctly, most of the ladies' preferred drink was Hennessy.

Even though I was not a heavy drinker, or smoked a lot of weed, I still indulged in it, and it was still sinful.

As I stated earlier there is no little sin or big sin, no little lie or white lie. All lies are from the prince of darkness, and God hates all sin and liars.

More than likely, most who read this particular chapter will say, or think, "God is a God of love and loves everybody. I just cannot believe that He would prepare a place of such torment, and then throw people into it to be tortured for all eternity. It's the cruelest thing I've ever heard of and I just can't believe it."

If that is your thought, it is somewhat true. God is a God of love, and He does love absolutely everyone. You are also correct in believing that He did not prepare a place of such torment for you, or I, but He did prepare it for Satan and all of his angels. Satan is the leader of a band of renegade angels, who, by there own free will, decided to join in his attempt to overthrow the Kingdom of God. When God sent Michael, his chief angel of war to throw Satan and his band of renegade angels out of heaven, He prepared a place of torment called hell; a nether place of turmoil where He would ultimately send Satan and all who have decided and will decide to follow him. This place of everlasting turmoil was not by any means, prepared for those who love the Lord and live by his commandments, but for Satan, his Angels, and all those who follow his path of evil. Therefore, if you follow the ways of Satan and not God, then you alone condemn yourself to hell and will reside there forever and ever.

Matthew, also known as Levi, before his conversion from a publican, or tax-gatherer under the Romans at Capernaum wrote in Matthew 6:24, "No man can serve two masters: for either he will hate the one, and love the other; or else he will hold to the one, and despise the other. Ye cannot serve God and mammon." Mammon is material wealth or possessions, which may, in many cases, have a debasing influence on those who possess them.

Matthew is extremely clear in the fact that he states no man, who without literally saying it meant that man or woman cannot serve two masters. He or she will hate one, and love the other, or be faithful to one and despise or look down on with contempt or aversion, a desire to avoid, the other.

The Apostle Peter, one of the faithful followers that walked with Jesus during His time here on earth wrote in 2nd Peter 3:9, "The Lord is not slack concerning his promise, as some men count slackness; but is longsuffering to us-ward, not willing that any should perish, but that all should come to repentance."

Believe me when I say that God is by no means slack in anything that He does or says He is going to do. Slackness is characterized by slowness, sluggishness, lacking in energy, or not using due diligence in taking care of business. God takes care of business concerning all things, especially the promises that he makes to us. If God says He is going to do something, promised or not, you can consider it done, no matter how long it takes.

The latter part of the above verse says that God is also not willing that any should perish. The key to this particular scripture is not willing that any should perish. This, however, does not mean that any will not perish… it is just not His will that any should perish.

Merriam-Webster's Dictionary defines the word willing as, (1) prepared in mind or by disposition, (2) consisting of or proceeding from an exercise of free will, (3) to be inclined, and (4) to give to another by will.

It is God's will that all, each and everyone of us come to repentance and seek His face for forgiveness for all sin through His son Jesus; the one and only way to everlasting life.

John, another beloved disciple that also walked with Jesus while He was here on earth writes in the book of Revelation 21:8, "But the fearful, and unbelieving, and the abominable, and the murderers, and whoremongers, and sorcerers, and idolaters, and all liars shall have their part in the lake which burneth with fire and brimstone: which is the second death."

Remember, God is not slack concerning His word so He must stand fast to all things that He has spoken. So, if you have not loved and served God to the best of your ability, Matthew writes in the latter verse of Matthew 25:41 that God will say to those unbelievers, "Depart from me, ye cursed, into everlasting fire, prepared for the devil and his angels."

Isaiah, an evangelical prophet of the Lord writes in the first part of Isaiah 5:14, "Therefore hell hath enlarged herself, and opened her mouth without measure."

God has no choice but to stand, and therefore be steadfast to His own word. Therefore, hell enlarges itself every day, allowing it to contain and accommodate all those who do not follow the righteous and narrow path of the Lord, and then die in their sin.

The book of Numbers, verse 23:19 reads, "God is not a man, that he should lie; neither the son of man, that he should repent: hath he said, and shall he not do it? Or hath he spoken, and shall he not make it good?"

If you want salvation and forgiveness from God, which can only be obtained through his faithful Son,

Christ Jesus, who was unmercifully beaten, shed His precious blood on the cross at Calvary, and then died for each and every one of us, all you have to do is ask.

Therefore, I shout with much gladness and thankfulness, saying, "Thank God for the blood of Jesus, which saves us all from all sin!" He is faithful to save, forgive us, and then bring us out of a life of darkness if we ask Him to. He brought me out of the miry clay, and He will bring you out, too, if you just ask.

Even though David and I both knew about God and the wage of sin, which is death, it was the last and farthest thing from our minds. We were interested in nothing but women, singing, and a record deal, to top it all off. We were lost, walking in darkness, and having a lot of fun.

Toward the end of that year, David and I went on an audition, located in the San Fernando Valley. These guys had some tight tracks, and all they needed were two more vocalists to complete the group.

They liked the way David and I sounded, so we ended up joining their group. We called ourselves, "A Touch Plus," and did mostly upbeat tunes with nicely choreographed dance steps. One of the songs I especially liked singing was, "Since I Lost My Baby," as recorded by Luther Vandross.

Since David had the best voice, he was the man out front. What can I say? When you're good, you're good! Yet, I found myself thinking, "Here I go again, singing background."

Even though I wanted to sing lead, I had concluded that singing background would be no problem because all I wanted was a record deal.

After that, once we were making big money, getting some worldwide recognition, and were well on our way to the big time, I would finally break out on my own.

About a month after recording, things began to look up and I could finally justify singing background, when we landed a publishing deal with Playful Music; a subsidiary of Warner Brothers Records.

I was finally on my way, I thought, but unfortunately, a few months later, we found out that the record company only wanted to use our talents for writing and had no intention on signing us as a new R&B act.

I was extremely upset and became very low in spirit. It seemed like, everything I tried to accomplish, just was not panning out for me. Even my job was not working.

I began to fall, sinking into a deep, dark depression. I started acting wild and doing all kinds of crazy things. Things got so bad that I wanted to die. Why was this happening to me? I made no money doing what I love to do, and it was killing me.

It was as though God intentionally sabotaged every effort I made to succeed, and I couldn't figure out or understand for the life of me, what was going on, and why.

Reggie Morris

Steve, Reggie, & Me in the studio recording "Time Seems To Fly"

Reggie, John, & Me

David in his Hollywood Suits

A-Touch-Plus

CENTER OF ATTRACTION

Eight

" A VISIT FROM THE HOLY SPIRIT "

One weekend, after I had finished partying, I drove to the beach, sat in my car, and looked out at the Pacific Ocean, thinking.

There is truly nothing in the world quite like sitting on the beach, looking out at the ocean. The feeling is unexplainable. It is strange how a body of water, that appears so calm and serene, can be so deadly and violent.

As I sat there staring at the ocean, I began crying out to God. I was tired of everything and every part of my life: the playboy lifestyle, sleeping around with different women, everything, the whole nine yards.
For me, that lifestyle had grown old quickly. I wanted something different. I had no idea at the time, but the purpose and plan God had already designed for my life was starting to surface; I just didn't realize it.

God was not going to let me succeed, not without Him being first in my life, but at that time in my life either I did not know what was going on, or I just did not want to believe or accept it. I thought I was losing it. I had even begun to think that I was going to be a loser in the music industry because nothing was working out. There was no one in my life that could help me but God, and I knew deep down in my spirit that I needed Him now like never before.

"Dear God," I whispered, "please help me. I don't know what else to do. I have tried everything, but nothing is working out. Everything I try seems to crumble right between my fingers. Lord, I need your help."

Suddenly, Atlanta Georgia was on my mind, and I had a strong desire to move there.

A week later, I was talking to my friend Tony Clemons, another party animal I used to run around with, about my sudden desire to move out of Los Angeles.

"Why don't you move to Atlanta?" he said, "I have a brother there who has a large house and you could stay with him until you get on your feet."

Well, as you might imagine, my lip literally dropped.

"This must be an act of God," I said, "because brotha', Atlanta, Georgia has been on my mind and in my spirit for an entire week now!"

Three months later, near the end of 1992, after completing an album with Playful Music, I sold my bed, and two black & white televisions to a couple of college students, and then packed my car with everything I could cram into it and moved to Atlanta.

Nine

"Georgia"

Once I arrived in Atlanta, I contacted a few of my old, high school classmates, who had moved there a few years earlier. We got together and they drove me around town, and hipped me on a few of the ins and outs of the city; the important things like where to go, as well as where and who to stay away from.

During it all, I discovered that Atlanta is rather slow compared to Los Angeles. However, it is definitely an up and coming city because so many people have moved there from various states, and other countries, due to the economical opportunities available to blacks and other minorities.

Two months later, I landed a daytime job, driving a shuttle bus for a Medicaid transportation company. Everything was going great, until an overwhelming feeling that something was still missing from my life came over me. It became so intense; I got on my knees and began talking to the Lord about it.

As I prayed, the telephone suddenly rang.

When I picked up the receiver, an old, high school classmate named Charrell pleasantly surprised me.

"Hey, Tony! What's going on?" She asked with a burst of energy.

"Not much. How about you," I quickly replied.

"Not much! I was just calling to invite you to my church."

I thought about it for a moment, and then said, "Sure!"

"Good," she quickly shouted, "The name of it is Hopewell Baptist Church. It's a small church that sits on top of a hill."

She told me a little more about the church, and then how to get there.

When I arrived at the church later that evening, it reminded me of one of those churches I used to see in movies. Not like the little, white steeple church with the white picket fence sitting on top of some hill, surrounded by green pastures, but in the sense that it actually sat on top of a hill and looked quiet and serene, and it had its own graveyard located in the rear for its members.

When I stepped inside the church, I saw that it was huge, and could easily seat around four hundred members and was completely full. I found my way to a seat as Pastor Sheals preached with what appeared to be every bit of strength in his body. I mean he was laying it down hard!

After he finished his sermon, he began praying; really praising God and it was starting to get to me. I could tell that the anointing of God was all over him. Up until then, I do not believe I had ever heard anyone preach the way Pastor Sheals preached that day.

Don't get me wrong, I'm not saying that the men of God where I grew up were not anointed, or ever preached a good sermon because they did; it was just that this was something different. This Pastor was explaining the Bible in a way that anyone, even a child could understand it. He had a way of

bringing the bible to life in a way that applied to how we as individuals live life today, and I could relate to what he was teaching. So much so, until God's Holy Spirit was drawing and reeling me in like a huge, fish at the end of a master fisherman's line, and I knew it. Not only did I know it, I was ready. I was ready for God to save me from the cold, heartless, warping influence of this world.

I was sick and tired of the way things were going in my life. Something had to change, and, I knew that I had to turn my life over to the care of Christ for that change to take place in a way that was conducive to a wholesome, moral way of life, and tonight was the night.

The next thing I knew, I was praying aloud, and praising God. I was completely submerged, praising and worshipping Him, and, for some reason, I just could not stop, nor did I want to. After a while, I found myself standing at the altar, asking God to forgive me for all of my sins. He did, and that same night I received His Holy Spirit.

After that night was over, I kept visiting Pastor Sheals' church, and then finally joined. I also joined the male chorus and sanctuary choir. I felt good because I knew I had finally made the right decision with my life.

Pastor William L. Sheals

Hopewell Baptist Church (The Miracle Hall)

Hopewell Baptist Church (The City of Hope)

Ten

" A New Life And A New Wife "

About a year had passed since I had given my life to the Lord, and I was now the proud owner of my own transportation business, which was a break from the shuttle job I had when I first arrived in Atlanta.

I transported Medicaid patients, mostly expecting mothers to various doctor appointments, using my own van.

Things were going well for me. I had moved into a nice apartment and opened an office with a friend/business partner. Business was booming, life was good, and my pockets were fat. There was only one thing missing, and that was the love of a woman. Not just any woman, though, I knew that I needed a wife. Since I had given my life to the Lord, I knew I could not play the field anymore nor even think about it, and I was getting lonely.

At this point, all Satan needed was a door, some way to get to me and lure me back into the world. If I was not careful, Satan could use the fact that I was lonely as a means of attack. He could send a woman into my life to comfort me, make feel loved and wanted, and then through the desires of lust, slowly lead me back to a life of sin.

Her name would probably be the most beautiful name my ears had ever heard, her skin smoother than silk, and softer than any cloud that God has placed in the heavens.

Unfortunately, however, her bed would lead to the pits of hell.

By any name, she is none other than Delilah, Satan's most powerful and widely used weapon of war in his arsenal of tricks in the war of principalities; a war between God and Satan for the souls of men.

One taste of her arousing, deliciously fatal kiss, the sweet potion of death, and old slew foot would find his way back into my life, divert me from God's purpose, and then send me spiraling out of control on the road of darkness. I knew that I did not want that. Therefore, the only reasonable and safe thing for me to do was to pray and ask God to send me a wife.

One day, one of my regular riders, a woman I transported to and from the doctor, told me of a sister she had who was coming to the states from Belize, Central America. She said that her name was Chris, and that she was looking for a caring, handsome man to marry, and I looked like the one.

"Okay," I said, "let me meet her when she gets in."

Four months later, Chris arrived in Atlanta. I set it up with her sister and met Chris a week before Valentine's Day. When she stepped out of the car with her mother and sister, I thought to myself; "Okay, she looks good, nice hair, nice complexion, not bad," but of course, being an entertainer, I have had beautiful women before so it wasn't really about all that.

The main thing for me, though, was to get out of fornication. That way, Satan could not keep me in bondage with sex because I would have my own wife: unless of course I fell into infidelity after marriage. You see, I believe the Bible, and I believe what it says.

Paul, a devout disciple of Jesus Christ wrote in the latter verse of 1st. Corinthians 7:1, "It is good for a man not to touch a woman." I suppose that was good for Paul, and anyone else who wanted to live that way of life, but I knew I was not going out like that; at least I didn't want to anyway.

Paul goes on to say in Corinthians 7:2, "Nevertheless, to avoid fornication, let every man have his own wife, and every woman have her own husband." So, I thought to myself, "Okay, father. Is this the one for me?"

As she approached my van with her sister and mother, I thought; "Okay, she has a nice walk." It was smooth and portrayed confidence, and I liked that.

When she finally reached my van, she immediately introduced herself and mother to me. She was very, soft-spoken with brown eyes, and I liked that about her, too. There was only one problem, though; she did not appear to be interested in me which, if I must say so myself, threw me, somewhat. Not that I thought I was all that, but I think I'm sort of charming, definitely tall, and some even think that I am fairly good-looking.

"God, are you sure this is the one for me?" I inquired of the Lord silently within myself, "Because she doesn't seem to be interested in me at all." I thought about it for a moment, and then asked her out on a date, and, to my surprise, she accepted.

A month later, Chris and I ended up in Florida, getting married. I could not believe it! I had actually gotten married! I was so excited I called all of my friends in Los Angeles, Florida, and Mississippi to tell them the good news, but they couldn't believe it, either, and were as shocked as I was.

"You've really changed," everyone said.

"Yeah, for the better," I replied.

There was only one thing, however, that had not changed about me, and that was my desire to be a successful recording artist.

A few months later, I decided to go back into the studio and record some new material. I wanted to do a few Rhythm and Blues tunes, and then shop them around town with the hopes of landing a record deal.

I began searching for a producer and soon found one with a nice studio. We produced three songs, titled the demo, "A Good Love," and then began looking for that record deal; yet, success still eluded me. Nobody was interested in my music and the entire process of trying to find a deal seemed increasingly impossible as the days turned into weeks, and the weeks into months.

It became quite frustrating, to say the least, but the word "quit" was not a part of my vocabulary.

Before I knew it, an entire year had passed and I was still looking for a deal, but I was not any closer to it than I was the year before. One day as I sat in my car totally frustrated, gorged with a mammoth sense of hopelessness, and completely burnt out, I cried out to God, "How come I can't get my music career off the ground? What am I doing wrong?"

I simply could not figure it out. I knew I was saved, and that in my heart I had turned my life over to Christ, but there was absolutely nothing I could do to make my dream of writing, singing, and recording songs for a living come true. Little did I know or understand that what I was still seeking were the pleasures of the world, and not the perfect and divine will of God in my life.

Tony's Non-Emergency Transportation Van

Tony & Chris

Chris

Tony, Chris, and Pastor Sheals

Tony and Chris

Valanji, Tawain(in back), Chris mother Mrs. Aguilar & Tony

Eleven

" A CHANGE OF HEART "

A few weeks had passed when, one Sunday afternoon while I was sitting in church, Pastor Sheals preached a sermon entitled, Are you doing what God wants you to do? As he preached, he kept looking at me or, at least, it felt as though he was. You know the feeling, right. You are sitting in church, the pastor is preaching, you are as guilty as sin, and the message feels as though it had been written for you and you alone. As far as I was concerned, that day his message had my name all over it or, at least, it felt as though it did. Everything that Pastor Sheals was preaching about that day seemed as though it was, directed toward me. There is no way he could have been speaking to anybody else.

When I finally made it home later that evening, I was an emotional wreck. My heart felt like a two-ton block of concrete. I did not even take the time to get on my knees to pray.

Instead, I just sat there on the living room sofa and began talking with the Lord as though He were sitting right next to me.

"Father," I cried loudly with complete abandonment to my own desires, "If you do not want me to sing rhythm and blues anymore, remove it from my heart right now!"

Then, just like that, it was gone! It felt like the Spirit of the Lord had consumed my entire body and then completely and instantly changed me. I suddenly had an intense desire to sing for Christ and no one else. I could barely believe what had just occurred. It was hard to fathom that my heart

and my mind had been, instantly transformed, literally in the twinkling of an eye. I was so excited about it that I called my family and friends to tell them about what had just happened to me, and they could not believe it either.

Over the next two or three years, everything seemed to be going great for my wife and I. I had totally surrendered everything in my life over to Christ: my will and my desires. I was living in the complete will of God and had no doubt, whatsoever, that things were going to get nothing but better, however, they didn't; they only got worse.

In fact, things just got terribly bad.

First, my transportation business started to go down the tubes because the State decided to drop the cost of transportation to barely nothing; purposely putting small transportation businesses out of business so that they could run the whole thing themselves.

Groups of small business owners like me got together and hired lawyers to fight back in court, to no avail; it was useless, and there was nothing we could do about it. We were trying to fight the very people who had made the laws and they were not trying to hear what we had to say or how we felt.

Secondly, the Internal Revenue seized everything I had, including my bank accounts, and then threatened to take my vans away. I simply could not believe that my world was crashing down again. This was something that I simply could not see coming. How could it happen? I was living the life and doing everything within my heart that I knew Christ wanted me to do. How could this be happening to me?

I fell on my face and again before the Lord, and this time, I literally screamed out to God in despair and desperation,

"No, no, no! Not again, Lord! Not again!"

***

The next thing I knew, I was struggling to pay the rent and the note on my Jeep. After a while, my wife and I decided to return the Jeep to the dealership before they decided to repossess it. I then found a part-time job, driving for another transportation company while Chris baby-sat a few times a week for our neighbors. It lasted a few months and we did not have very much money coming in, but every single dime we acquired was definitely a big help.

***

One day, as I was sitting at the table looking over the bills, wondering how I was going to pay them, Chris said to me, so sweet and tenderly with that deep, Belizean accent of hers, "Babesman," she said.

Babesman is the pet name she gave me when we first met, "don't fret. Things gonna' work out, Mun! I can feel it, Mun!"

It is hard to explain, but those few words coming from Chris felt and made me feel so good. It felt good to know that she still had my back, regardless of how bad things had gotten for us. It was not long after, however, before we had begun to feel the depression and pressure of everything all over again.

One night, while I was in my living room, I began talking to God as though he were sitting in the chair next to me.

"God, please help me, Father!" I cried, as tears gently began falling from my eyes. "You said that you would never leave me, nor forsake me, Jesus! You said this in your word!" Then, I shouted loudly, "Please help me! Now!"

***

That next day, as I was driving along the freeway, returning home from dropping a friend off, a strange thing occurred. Some of you might not believe what I am about to tell you, but it is true. Right before my eyes, right there in the midst of the deep, blue sky, I literally saw a window open. As it did, a pair of hands appeared within the window, holding something. Suddenly, a white dove flew from the hands into the sky. I was aghast and in full-blown awe of what my eyes had just beheld.

"Lord, what is this?" I humbly asked, and then, suddenly, I heard a powerful voice.

"I want to bless all my children on the earth with these blessings I have on the shelves behind me. Look and see!"

When I looked, I saw miles and miles of shelves with sparkles on them, and then I heard the voice again, "I cannot bless my children with these blessings because they are not ready to receive them."

I was speechless! I sat there in my car trying to determine if I was daydreaming. Then I suddenly snapped back to reality and realized that I was parked alongside the freeway with absolutely no recollection of how I got there, or ever pulling over, but I felt so good inside. I felt so good that I just sat there with my hands waving back and forth in the air, crying, and praising God for what He had shown me.

People, who were speeding by in their cars, must have thought I was crazy the way I was shouting and howling, but I didn't care. God Himself had just showed me something wonderful; something that literally blew my mind.

About a week later, while I was sitting in church, praying, the Holy Spirit began speaking to me. As He did, a strong feeling, urging me to move back to Los Angeles suddenly came over me. I prayed about it for a few weeks, and then finally spoke with my pastor about it.

"Just make sure that you are hearing from God," he urged, "because the devil can be very tricky, and deceitful."

I prayed and fasted some more, but the feeling just kept getting stronger, so I finally spoke with Chris about it.

"I'll go wherever you go, Babesman," she said so compassionately, "as long as God told you to do it."

After that, we began saving money, and soon had enough to rent a U-haul truck, and before we knew it, we were on our way back to Los Angeles.

Twelve

" THE NEW ME "

When Chris and I arrived in Los Angeles, my old friends, the ones I used to hangout, party, and run the streets with were glad to see me, and eagerly waiting to get started right were we left off with womanizing, club hopping, and drinking, but my life and personality had completely changed, and they could tell.

The producer, whom I had met and worked with several years earlier, didn't want to work with me any more, and some of my friends didn't want to sing or hang out because they said I was trying to be, too Holy!

That is the way it is when you truly change your way of life and begin living and doing the will of God. You will find out who your true friends really are. You will find that many of the people that called themselves your friends through thick and thin really were not your friends at all.

A true friend will love you unconditionally, regardless of your religious preference and way of life. This does not mean that if you are saved, sanctified, and filled with God's precious Holy Spirit you need to hang out with someone who was a true friend when you were both in the world, and doing the things of the world. It merely means that a true friend, even though he or she has changed their life and now lives for Christ, should always be there for an old, friend, in a supportive way, if the need should arise.

A true friend should especially be doing everything possible, within his or her capacity, to draw that Soul to Christ. However, this type of relationship, spiritual

intervention, and friendship must at all costs, be handled with studious care, and only when the threat of losing one's own salvation is of no issue.

You may even find that some of your truest friends may not even believe in God and, in fact, may even be atheists, unbelievers in Christ, which is just an opportunity for you as a believer in the sanctified blood of Jesus to do your very best to win them over to Christ.

"My life has changed," I told them, "I can no longer do the things I used to do, and I cannot go to those kinds of places anymore. I can't even hang out."

I knew that I could not be around certain people or hang out with some of my old friends because God had made a change in my life, and I knew that He no longer wanted me to associate myself with certain people or their environments. I knew that God had sent me back to Los Angeles for a reason, and that He wanted to use me for His glory, and most of all, I knew I wanted to let Him.

A few months later, I landed a job and started looking for a studio to record another CD, but this time it would be a Gospel CD. After going to about six studios, I finally came across one with a young producer named Sa Ra Chris, whose tracks were bangin'," off the hook; you know, really good.

I explained to him the kind of music I wanted to do.

"No problem," he said, "I can produce any kind of music you want my brother!"

Sa Ra Chris and I immediately went into the studio and went to work. We were pumping out tunes left and right. Sa Ra Chris was the best producer I had run into yet, and his prices were more than affordable; praise God! I felt completely assured within my spirit that God had definitely led me to this brother.

Finally, something good was taking place in my life once again. We were recording song after song, trying to finish my CD before the end of the year.

Just as things were looking up, for a change, I received a call from home saying that my grandmother had died. That phone call really hurt me because I was looking forward to her hearing one of my favorites on the CD entitled Trouble in My Way. I had spoken with her a few times regarding some of the songs.

She told me that she was glad about the project and was looking forward to seeing and hearing me sing it to her when I came home. Unfortunately, I did not finish recording in time. Life is so unpredictable.

You just never know what to expect from one day to the next, and there was definitely more to come.

A month later, my closest aunt, Myrtle Jean

Anderson Davis, also went home to be with the Lord. I was crazy about her. She had the kind of smile that reminded me of an Angel. She was a very friendly person, who loved the Lord and would always bring something to our house whenever she came by. I wrote a song in her memory and entitled it, Angel Gone Home.

At one point, shortly after my Aunt Myrtle Jean's death, I was sitting at my mother's kitchen table, crying, deeply missing my aunt when the Holy Spirit spoke to me, saying, "Please, don't worry. Please, don't cry. The angel from heaven has gone back home to be with the Lord, and we shall meet again one day."

Auntie Martyle

Auntie Martyle's kids
Terry & Troy

1 9 9 8
"Lord I Thank You"

Singles
"TROUBLE IN MY WAY" & "ANGEL GONE HOME"

Thirteen

" MY FIRST GOSPEL VIDEO "

In February 1998, I completed my first gospel CD and called it, "Lord, I Thank You," because God had given me the strength I needed and carried me through so much pain, hurt, and sadness. I was thankful to Jesus for carrying me through the making and molding. In fact, He is still making and molding me.

Over the next two years as I advertised the CD, I met a wonderful woman named Vicki Lee, the founder of, "Saints of Value Ministries," a gospel Ministerial Training Center. Sister Vicki is truly a devout, Holy Ghost-filled woman of God that loves the Lord. The very first time I appeared on her cable show, I felt the presence of the Holy Spirit consuming the atmosphere around her and the entire building.

She was so real, and her show was unlike any other local cable show I had ever seen or appeared on; truly anointed, and contained a strong message of salvation for its viewers.

Months later, I took my gospel, singing ministry to another level by being ordained as a minister in music. While conducting one of my classes, I met a wonderful, kind, crazy about the Lord brother named Ron Roberson. We had spoken a year earlier about doing a Gospel music video on one of the songs from my CD, but I did not have the money to pay him. During class one night, I noticed that he kept looking at me.

One night, he suddenly stood up in front of the entire class and said God had told him to bless me by doing a

Gospel video for me, and the best part of the blessing was that it would not cost me a dime. I was ecstatic, to say the least. God had once again given me favor for being obedient and trying to do a good work for his kingdom.

My second CD began in March 2001. After much prayer, I decided to do a new CD, but this time I wanted to have some anointed singers with me who knew and lived by the word of God.

Again, after much prayer, and the faithful guidance of the Holy Spirit, I began searching for singers that God would use along with me to bring forth His praise through song.

It did not take long before God blessed me with some wonderful, anointed saints, who loved Him as much as I did. Their names were Philip Coleman, Martha Hardwell, and Tonya Davis, the background singers on my second CD entitled, I Must Tell Jesus.

We sang a few songs from the CD in September 2001 at a local church in Inglewood, True Vine Baptist Church, pastured by Reverend, Austin F. Williams.

Before that wonderfully successful night, I had approached three other churches with the hopes of having a release celebration, but Reverend Williams was the only one who opened his doors to us. I was disappointed in the other churches because I had faithfully supported them in the past, and they had told me that they would be there for me when I needed them, but weren't. Thank God for favor! The release celebration concert at Reverend Williams' church was awesome!

My third project was released Christmas 2002. It was a two-song CD called, This Christmas. It was something I wanted to do just to make people smile. The songs were very familiar, loved, and known around the world. Included were This Christmas by Donnie Hathaway, who was definitely one

of the most influential singers of all time, and Chestnuts by the great Nat King Cole, another very influential crooner that had a voice that was truly as smooth as silk. As much as I liked the project and thought that it was quite good, I must say that I was quite surprised to find that it had even sold a few copies in Japan.

The fourth CD began in November 2002. I went to the studio to pick up some fresh tracks from Sa Ra Chris. I started writing and singing to one of the melodies, I was working on when, suddenly, my voice started cracking, and I felt a cold coming over me. I decided to give my voice a rest for about a month, which turned into a couple of months. During that time, Sa Ra Chris had to leave town. It would not be until after the Christmas holidays before I got back to work on the songs.

After I got back into the swing of things and began putting the final changes on, A Better Day, my voice began giving me problems again. I decided to call Damien Lawson, a young gifted brother, whom I had met through his uncle, Curtis Mickle, and asked him to work with me on the project. I loved his style of singing and he had a fresh sound, which was something I had not heard in a while.

"Okay," he said without question, and then we immediately went to work and the first song was completed. Once the song was completed, I decided to see a throat specialist, who told me that I had small, seedy nodes on my vocal cords that required surgery to correct the sinus problems it was causing.

"No way," I thought, "how could this be happening?"

I wanted and needed to finish this CD, which only consisted of three songs before the summer arrived, but the condition with my throat only got worse. It had gotten so bad

until I finally made an appointment to have the operation.

I wanted to have it done immediately so I could get back to work on the CD, but the doctor said it would be better to wait until around August. That way it would allow enough time, along with the steroids that he was going to prescribe, for the swelling go away.

Around the first part of March 2003, I began talking to God about the CD.

"God, I would love to do this CD with some brothers that are true believers, and love you as much as I do." I said, "I would like to sing with some anointed brothers this time. So Father God, please bless me with some real, true brothers."

A few weeks later while I was in prayer, the Holy Spirit brought a brother named David B. before my face. David B. had sung at my second CD release party.

I called his record label and spoke with Quake, the

label's president, who is also a very good friend. I explained to him exactly what I wanted to do.

"Tony, man, you are good people," he said, "I know you try to do the right things so go ahead and give David B. a call. I won't hold him back from doing good things."

A few days later, I phoned David B. and told him what I wanted to do and that Quake said everything was cool.

"Man, I don't know if I want to be a part of a group situation. I'm mainly a solo artist," he said, "but still, let me hear the tracks."

After I took him a copy of a couple of tracks to check out, he phoned me two days later saying, "Man, those tracks are slammin'," he shouted.

"What direction are you trying to go?"

I told him what God had placed in my heart to do.

"If God is in it, so am I," he said, "Check it out, though, I don't mind helping out with the song, brother Tony, as long as there are no contracts involved."

" No problem, brother David. That sounds fair, and besides, I'm paying for all the studio time as well."

I also mentioned that I was trying to get another friend, Damien, who co-wrote one of the songs to sing with us.

A week later, I asked Damien three times about

singing with me, but he had absolutely no interest in singing with a group.

I asked him to pray about it and see what God had to say about him singing with me, but he said, "I could pray about it, but I can already tell you that I'm just not interested in singing with a group."

"Okay," I said, "I can respect your decision."

Even though Damien did not say it, I knew he thought that he was better than I was, vocally, that is, and, to be honest, he was, and still is. This was not about being better, or who sounded the best. It was about doing a good work for the Lord, and that was all that was important to me: pleasing God.

I decided to ask another friend about singing with us, but before I did, I told David B. what Damien said about singing with us.

"Let me talk to him," he urged, "Because this is something big that God is doing."

A few days later, David, and I met with Damien and talked things over. We told him that this was something bigger than any one of us, and that God was doing something on a scale bigger than anything our natural eyes could see.

"I don't see it that way," Damien said, "I'm just not interested in being a part of a group."

That was the end of it. David and I left Damien with no hard feelings. As we did, I mentioned another singer I knew named Tony Novel, who had sung with me a few years earlier.

When I called Tony and talked about what David B. and I wanted to do, his response was pretty much the same as Damien's, in that, he was mainly a solo artist, but he would be willing to try to work with us because he knew that the tracks were slamming.

What he really wanted, though, was to meet my producer and get his own thing going. Of course, I had no problem with that. While he was working with us, I just wanted to put in one hundred percent and do things right.

I wanted no less than his very best effort put forth on the project, regardless to what his hidden agenda might have been.

We all agreed to try to work together to put together a couple of tracks for a CD, and then immediately went into the studio and began working on the material. We soon realized, however, that things were not working out. Tony just could not seem to work with us in a way that made him a part of the team, and teamwork was what we needed to even stand a chance of becoming a successful group. It was as he said; he just really did not want to be a part of group.

I became a little frustrated and decided to talk things over with Damien one more time.

I knew that it would be easier for a group to obtain a record deal with a major label than it would be for a single artist.

Damien's response, however, was still no.

At that point, David said "Let me pray about it

and ask God for some guidance."

A week later while I was sitting at the dining room table, I overheard a young man singing from outside my apartment.

He sounded so good that I got up to check it out, and as I did, the telephone rang.

When I answered the phone, it was David B.

"Step outside," he said, "I want you to meet a brother I've known since back in the day. His name is DeFrantz Forrest, and his father is Gene Chandler, the legendary "Duke of Earl.""

"Yeah, okay... I'll be right out."

I hung up the telephone, and then walked to the front door in anticipation of meeting whoever this young man was. He had already peaked my interest with his smooth voice. When I opened the front door, he was still singing as he sat in the driver's seat of a white S.U.V. David B. was sitting next to him in the passenger's seat.

I walked over to the S.U.V. and David B. said, "This is DeFrantz, the new member of our group, who I told you about a couple of days ago. What do think?"

"He sounds cool," I replied.

I looked at DeFrantz and asked, "Did you hear any of our tracks?"

"Yeah, man...they sound tight," he said.

"Okay, brother. Let's do this."

David B. and DeFrantz got out of the S.U.V. and walked over to the passenger side of the car were I was standing. After a few moments, we joined hands and began to pray.

As we were praying, I mentioned to them that I was having some problems with my voice, and that my doctor had advised me to have nasal surgery to correct a sinus condition that was causing my vocal problems. David B., and DeFrantz immediately laid hands on my throat and began praying right there on the spot.

After we finished, we went into the house and talked about the group for a while. As we did, DeFrantz asked, "What are we going to call ourselves?"

"Let's pray about it," I suggested, "and see what God says."

We all agreed the name would be, anointed, and then David and DeFrantz got up and left.

A couple of weeks later after we rehearsed a few times, we agreed to call our group, D.D.T., the acronym for David, DeFrantz, and Tony.

***

Around the end of April, after rehearsing, we went into the studio and recorded, A Better Day, which came out great. Everyone, including our producer Sa Ra Chris, was pleased with what we had achieved in such a short time.

The following month, we went back into the studio and recorded, All right-All right. We were really surprised with how well the recordings were turning out, considering we had only been singing together for no more than a month. Of course, we knew deep down in our spirits that God had put us together to sing for His Glory.

For me, it was such a blessing because David B. and DeFrantz were excellent singers, and the best part of all, as far as the studio work was concerned, was that I did not have to tell or show them how to be creative with the songs. It just came natural to them. They were the kind of artists I had longed to work with.

"God is so good," I whispered to myself.

***

In June, we went into the studio to record our final song for the demo, and called it, Never Give Up. A few days later, we mixed and mastered all three songs, and then began shopping for a record deal. We were all excited about it, too. We knew in our hearts that God had brought each one of us together to do a good work in His holy name, and that our efforts were blessed from the very beginning.

I was especially happy because God had done what I had asked Him to do, up to this point, and fueled me with energy and aspiration.

Now all I needed was for Him to show up and show out

again by blessing D.D.T. with a record deal.

He is like that, you know, a show off. God is a big show off, and loves doing it. Just give Him the opportunity and He will literally blow your mind. Of course, most flamboyant individuals like to show off, and I cannot truly think of anyone more flamboyant than God. Let's face it, His streets are paved with gold, His throne is adorned with every kind of precious stone imaginable. There are jeweled crowns for all his saints and the wise men, which sit around His throne praising Him continuously, and for those who make it into His kingdom's mansion.

A few days later, we began praying and laying hands on the CDs, asking Jesus to touch every one of them, and to lead them into the right hands. Not only did we desperately want a record deal, but most of all; we wanted every song on the CD to be a blessing to everyone who listened to our music. From that point on, while we did everything within our power to push the CD, we sat back, waiting for the songs to begin selling and the offers to start rolling in. Success, however, continued to elude the group.

I have since learned and now know, beyond a shadow of doubt, that God has His own way of doing things, and what he does for every individual, on a one-to-one basis is all done according to the heart of that man or woman. No matter how hard or how much we try to make things work out the way we want them to, God will still do things His way.

Paul, who was known as Saul before he came to the Lord said in Romans 8:27, "And He that searcheth the hearts knoweth what is the mind of the Spirit, because He maketh intercession for the saints according to the will of God."

This is simply saying that know matter what you say or try to make others think about you and your intentions, God

knows what is really on your mind. If you, who are saints, attempt to do something within the will of God, and Satan tries to block or hinder it, know that God will step in and work things out for you. He has not only searched your heart, and, knows your intentions, but He has also searched the heart of those trying to come against you. Romans 8:27, teaches us this very truth.

Nevertheless, some things occur in our lives that can make us think that God is looking the other way and not paying attention or concerned about our particular situation. We must know, however, that whatever way He manipulates or allows Satan to manipulate our lives that all things work according to God's perfect will, and are always working for our good; if we love God. This is the key to having things work for our good, loving God.

We must love Him, who first loved us. This, of course, is not to say that God does not occasionally, according to His own will and perfect plan, work things out for sinners as well.

We, who love God, have a promise from God himself that if we love Him, all situations, whether they be good or bad, are working for our good.

Romans 8:28 reads, "And we know that all things work together for the good of them that love God, to them who are called according to his purpose." This is a promise from God to those that love Him. To try to understand how a catastrophic occurrence in a person's life can work out for their good in the end is a futile, overwhelming waste of mind power.

This can be proven in the book of Isaiah when The Holy Spirit inspires Isaiah in the fifty-fifth chapter of the self-titled book Isaiah, verses eight and nine to write, "For my thoughts are not your thoughts, neither are my ways your ways, saith the Lord. For as the heavens are higher than the earth, so are my ways higher than your ways, and my thoughts than your thoughts."

No matter how hard we try, we could never figure out God's plan or His way of doing things in our lives. We, as believers in word of God, simply must believe and stand fast with every ounce of faith we can muster. We must believe that painful, catastrophic events in our lives and the lives of family and friends eventually work out for the good because God's holy word says it will.

Five nights later, after gang members gunned me down, while I was on my way to pick up my wife from work, our prayers for spiritual and material blessings turned into prayers for God's divine, life-saving intervention.

Pastor Vickie Lee
(Founder of Saints of Value Ministries)

Tony's Ordination Service

Pastor Vickie Lee and Tony
(S.O.V. Ordination Service)

Gospel sensation Anna Moore
& Tony at his Ordination Service

Martha, Pastor Johnson, Tonya, and Mr. Coleman

Tony Davis & New Praise

Pastor Dr. A .F. Williams
"TRUE VINE BAPTIST CHURCH"
Inglewood California

Pastor Ron Roberson, his wife, Tina, & Kezyah

2002
" This Christmas "

" THIS CHRISTMAS " CD

Tony, DeFrantz, and David B.

Fourteen

" THE GOOD SAMARITAN "

It was a beautifully warm, summer night, and the moon was full, lighting up the sky with a tranquil, translucent glow.

I was in my Jeep, Grand Cherokee, listening to some Gospel music while on the way to pick up Chris from work. She worked the swing shift in East Los Angeles caring for mentally challenged adults.

As I drove, I suddenly heard a telephone ringing in the background, and quickly realized that it was my cell phone.

I turned down the music, grabbed the phone located on the center console, pushed the talk button, and then placed the phone to my ear; it was Chris.

"Hello," I said, while keeping my eyes fixed on the road ahead.

"Hey, Babesman," she replied with her heavy Belizean accent.

"Oh, hey, Chris. I'm on my way to pick you up now."

"Okay, but I was wondering if you could go and pick up Keda for me? You know, the girl who is supposed to relieve me. Her car stopped a few blocks from here and she's got her boyfriend, his niece, and her little girl with her."

It had been a long day and I was tired, having done a lot of running around earlier, so I decided I would give Chris sort of a hard time before agreeing.

"Man, Chris, you know I have to go to work tomorrow. I'm tired!"

"I know, but she doesn't have any other way to get here. It's just a couple of blocks from here."

I thought about it for a moment, knowing that I was already going to do it, and then I reluctantly agreed.

"Yeah, okay. Tell me exactly where she is."

***

When I made it to the location where Keda's car had stopped, I pulled closer and saw Keda, the two little girls, and her boyfriend, I got out of my Jeep and walked up to their car.

"Hey, Chris called my cell and told me that you guys needed a ride."

"Yeah. Thanks for coming," Keda replied with a smile. "My car broke down again as you can see. I guess it's about time for a new one."

I thought to myself, "Yeah, you're telling me."

Keda, her boyfriend "E", and the two little girls got out of her broken down vehicle and walked over to my Jeep. Being the gentleman that I am or, at least, that I try to be, I opened the rear door for "E," and the two little girls. As they piled into the Jeep, Keda walked over to me. "This is my boyfriend, "E," she said.

By that time, "E" had buckled the two little girls safely in their seat belts, and then turned to me.

"Hey, how's it goin', Brother man?" I asked.

"It's ah-ight, He replied."

Finally, after I got in, buckled myself in, and started the Jeep, we were on our way.

Chris' job was just a block away and, besides the arguing that Keda and "E" was doing, everything else seemed fine. Soon we would be at Chris' job and Keda could relieve her, and then Chris and I would soon be at home in bed.

A few minutes later, as I prepared to make a right turn, I suddenly heard the sound of gunfire and it was coming from all around me.

"Oh Lord, somebody's shooting!" I yelled frantically.

"It sounds like they're shooting at us! Oh my God," Keda shouted.

In the back seat, the children just sat frozen with their eyes bucked wide open in terror.

I pressed harder on the gas and sped away.

***

A block away from where the shooting occurred, I pulled over to the right side of the street, and parked at the further end of the corner, and then proceeded to make sure everyone was okay; especially the two children.

"You all right?" I quickly asked Keda, "You didn't get hit, did you?"

Her voice trembled, as she replied, "No, I'm all right. I'm just worried about the kids."

We both turned and looked in the back seat to check on her boyfriend and the kids. The children were still sitting quietly in their seats, frozen with fear.

"Are you guys okay?" Keda asked.

"Yeah, mom," they replied.

"Is everybody okay?" I asked.

"Yeah, we're all right," E, replied, "they're just scared. To tell you the truth, so am I."

Keda asked "E" to pass her daughter to her. As he did, I turned around in my seat and looked around, still quite shaken, myself.

"Oh my God," I said, "I can't believe that those guys were shooting at us! Maybe we got caught in a cross fire!"

I kept looking around, just in case they were shooting at us on purpose, and then it hit me.

"I think a bullet hit my door," I shouted.

It was at that point when I noticed that my windshield was fogging up.

"Ah, man," I yelled in frustration, "I don't believe it! I think they hit my radiator!"

I was furious! Once I realized that everyone was all right, I picked up my cell phone.

"I'd better call the police," I blurted, and then dialed 9-1-1.

A few moments passed as the phone rang on the other end, and then finally someone answered.

"9-1-1, emergency. May I help you?" the operator asked.

"Yeah, my name is Tony Davis, and somebody just shot at us! They shot up my Jeep!"

"You say someone just shot at you and shot up your Jeep?"

"Yeah."

"Could you please give me your location?" she quickly asked.

After I gave her my location, and where I could be found, I walked back to where the shooting occurred to check on my wife and make sure that she was okay.

***

I ran up to the door and pounded on it a couple of times. Seconds later, Chris opened the door and I forced my way inside.

"What's the matter?" she asked hysterically.

"This is it," I yelled, "This is why I didn't want you working over here in the first place!"

"I knew it," she said, "I knew they were shooting at you guys. I could feel it!"

"Those fools shot up my jeep!"

"Oh my God, no! Are you okay?"

"That's it! I won't be coming back over here!"

I looked Chris, square in the eyes.

"I want you to get away from over here," I yelled. "Why this lady opened this type of facility over here, I will never understand! This is not the kind of neighborhood to open a board and care facility."

Chris immediately got on the telephone and called the lady who ran the boarding house to tell her that she was quitting, and I could not have been happier.

After that, I paced the floor, continuing to fuss as I waited anxiously for the police to arrive.

About fifteen minutes later, there was a knock at the front door. Chris walked to the door and looked through the peephole.

"It's the police," she said.

"Yeah, I called them."

Chris opened the door and let them in. I guess they could tell by the frustrated look on my face that I was the victim because one of them asked, "So, what happened, Mr. Davis?"

"I was on my way here to pick up my wife," I quickly answered, "when all of a sudden somebody started shooting at us!"

The police officers asked me a few more questions and I told them everything that I could remember. After I finished, they headed across the street to question a few guys who were standing outside in front of a house, just a few houses down from the shooting.

***

There were about four thugs standing around. One of the officers asked, "Did anyone see what happened?"

"No," one of the thugs quickly answered, "I heard the gunfire, but I didn't see where it was coming from."

I could tell by the way he answered the questions that he was lieing through his teeth. I knew he saw what had happened. I could feel it, and for all I knew, he probably had something to do with it.

"You mean to tell me that you guys didn't see anything?" the other officer asked, in disbelief.

The thugs looked at each other for a moment, and then one of them said, "Nah, we didn't see nothin'."

That's when I stepped in. I was upset and had heard all of the lies I wanted to hear. Somebody was going to tell the truth.

"Come on you guys," I pleaded. "I come over here every night to pick up my wife. Somebody saw somethin'!"

Both police officers' shook their heads, knowing they were lying, but what could they do. Nobody could prove they saw or heard anything. One of the officers turned to me and asked, "Can you take us to your vehicle?"

"Yeah, sure, no problem," I answered.

***

When the police officers and I arrived at my Jeep, "E" was on a cell phone. It wasn't until later that I found out he had called a relative to come pick up the kids.

The police officers began looking my Jeep over. As they did, I pointed out the bullet hole in my driver's door.

"This was caused by a nine-millimeter handgun," said one of the officers.

"A nine-millimeter," I exclaimed.

"That's right. Did you see who was shooting at you?"

"No, I didn't," I replied.

Suddenly, my cell phone rang. I took it out of my pocket, looked at the Caller ID and it was Chris, so I answered it.

"Hello."

"Hey, Babesman," she said.

"What's up, Chris?"

"I just saw this young guy come back to the house across the street on a bicycle," she replied, "He was over there earlier. I saw him run out of the house and get in a car by himself and drive off after the shooting ended!"

"Okay, hold on, I'll tell the police."

As the policeman still looked over my vehicle, I took the phone from my ear and cried, "It's my wife. She said one of the guys she saw run from across the street and drive away in a car, just came back on a bicycle!"

"Tell her to watch the house," one of the policemen replied, "If he comes out again, tell her to call you immediately."

I relayed the officer's message. "The police want you to watch the house and if he comes out again, call me immediately."

"Why won't they go over there and bring him out now?" she shouted through the phone.

"My wife wants to know why can't you go over

there and bring him out now."

"We can't enter without a search warrant," one of the officers explained.

Chris overheard the officer's response, got upset, and then yelled so loudly through the cell phone, you could probably hear her a block away.

"Aren't the bullet holes in the Jeep, warrant enough?"

I thought it was a valid question, myself, so I asked the cops the same thing.

"Aren't the bullet holes, warrant enough?"

One of the cops shook his head and said, "No, I'm sorry, but they're not."

I couldn't understand why, but I told Chris what he said, anyway. I told her that I would call her back when I got more information, and then after saying, "Good by," hung up the phone.

As I clicked off my cell phone, one of the officers announced, "If you'd like, we can phone Triple-A to come and pick up your vehicle.

In the meantime, we'll go back to where the shooting took place and do a little more investigating."

I thought about what he said for a moment, and I was sure that he could tell from my facial expression that I was not comfortable with his suggestion.

"Don't worry," he said, "everything's gonna' be

okay. Another unit's on its way here, as we speak."

The officer glanced at his watch and said, "They should be here any minute now."

"Are you sure," I asked, "because I really don't feel too safe in this area."

"Everything will be okay, Mr. Davis. We'll only be gone for a few minutes ourselves."

"You sure?" I asked nervously.

"I assure you, we'll be back within minutes."

Still, though, I was not comfortable with the officer's decision to leave me there without protection.

"Yeah, okay," I replied reluctantly.

The cops got in their squad car. As they drove away, me, Keda, and "E" sat on the curb near my Jeep, and began to wait.

Fifteen

" LITTLE VIETNAM "

Ten minutes later, as we sat on the curb waiting, a Triple-A truck turned the corner and slowly headed in our direction. Man, was I glad to see it.

I quickly jumped to my feet and began waving at the driver, who, after a moment, noticed me.

Just as the tow truck slowly continued toward us, it seemed as though the entire environment shifted into slow motion, as gunfire erupted all around us.

All I could hear was gunfire, coming from behind me; sounding off loudly in rapid repetition. It sounded like I was in Vietnam. Even though I knew that I wasn't, and that I was in the good ole U.S of A, I was definitely in the middle of a war zone at home.

It seemed as though everything continued moving in slow motion as I looked over at Keda and "E," who were scrambling for cover. Then, just as I turned to see who was shooting at us, a bullet tore into my left thigh. My leg felt like it was on fire! Then, another bullet ripped into the same thigh, and then another. The pain was excruciating! I could feel the air from more bullets as they whizzed by with daunting speed on both sides of my face and arms, barely missing me.

As the horror continued, I looked up and saw the Triple-A truck driver, who was stunned at what was happening. As he stared on in disbelief and dismay, four bullets suddenly bored into the front of his truck.

Frightened for his life, he threw his truck into reverse and began driving backwards, erratically; hitting two parked cars. He then slammed the truck into drive and sped away, burning rubber.

The pain in my leg kept growing, and growing, and growing. The feeling was like nothing I had ever felt in my entire life, and then I noticed that everything was suddenly quiet. The shooting had stopped, and I was sure that it was over.

The pain in my leg was so severe that all I could do was sit down on the ground beside the driver's door of my Jeep. No sooner than I had, the shooting started again. The gunfire was coming from seemingly every direction possible. The war had started all over again and now I was completely in the open.

As gunfire rang throughout the atmosphere, another shooter suddenly appeared a few feet in front of me, closer to the corner, and hiding behind a tree. He fired a shot, hitting me in my right thigh. I thought, "Is this nightmare ever going to end?"

With my body wounded and wracked with relentless pain, I tried to move toward the back of my Jeep, crawling on the ground as though I were in a real war zone, and I was, only I didn't have a weapon to return fire.

The bullets kept flying and I didn't think I was going to make it. As I kept crawling for my life in a futile effort to take cover, one of the bullets ricocheted off the ground and struck me in the lower part of my right calf, and then continued straight through, exiting at the top of my calf. I grabbed my leg in agonizing pain. Blood was everywhere; all over my face, hands... everywhere.

The pain grew intensely, but the strange part of it all was that I was more emotionally hurt than anything else. At least that was how I felt in my heart. I simply could not believe that someone was actually shooting at me. I cried with a loud, alarming voice, "Oh my God! No!"

As I cried out to God, I turned, looking over the front of my Jeep, and saw one of the shooters more clearly. He was slowly approaching, remaining slightly covered by a tree, but moving closer, and closer, and closer. I could not believe my eyes. He was just a boy, maybe seventeen or eighteen years old and his eyes were cold, black, and heartless.

Anger suddenly began to consume me and then, for that moment, I no longer cared what happened to me and I managed to rise to my feet. My clothes were soaked with blood. In fact, I looked as though I had bathed in blood.

My pant legs were completely red, literally drenched with my life giving force. I began yelling at the young man with everything in me.

"Hey, man," I screamed with violent anger, "What have I done to you to make you do this to me! Do you know me?" I asked! "I haven't done anything to you! " You will not shoot me anymore in the name of Jesus! I shouted.

Those words spilled out without me even thinking about it because my Spirit knew that by calling out the name of Jesus, the devil would flee and a bad situation could be turned around.

The boy merely looked at me with his cold, black, vacant, unsympathetic eyes, and then raised his gun and pointed it directly at my head.

I screamed at him again, "Now you want to kill me!

You've already messed me up! If killing me is going to make your life better than what it is, then go ahead!

A few moments passed as the boy continued pointing his gun toward my head, but I wasn't afraid and yelled at him again.

"If killing me is gonna' make your life better than what it is right now, go ahead!"

At that very instant, his hand suddenly began to tremble, and then he lowered the gun. As he did, I began drifting, semi-conscious from the immense loss of blood, and then fell to the ground.

As I lay there on the ground trying to pull myself together, I could feel myself slipping away, slipping into death's relentless, never-ending grasp, but I was determined to keep my eyes open, my mind focused and alert. I was going to stay alive.

A few seconds later, I began crawling toward the other side of the street, trying to find help, but there was none.

No one was around, at least not anyone who was willing to get involved, or help me, and that is the way it is in the world today. Nobody wants to get involved, even when someone's life is on the line.

Once I realized that I was on my own, and that no one was going to help me, I began thinking about my wife, wondering if I would ever see her again, or if this was it.

I wondered if this was my last night to live. I felt as though I could feel death creeping into my body and seeping into my mind.

I struggled to pull out my cell phone, which felt like it

was stuck in the pocket of my trousers." After, what seemed like an eternity, I was finally able to free it from my pocket, turned it on, and then punch in Chris' number. I could not understand why everything seemed to be taking so long. First, it seemed like forever before I was able to get my phone out of my pocket to dial Chris' number, and then it seemed like ages before I could hear it ringing on the other end, but I thanked God, when it finally did.

Chris answered the phone immediately, and man was it good to hear her voice, but I was getting so weak from the loss of blood that I could barely speak. Somehow, with every ounce of strength left in me, and with paramount urgency, I whispered her name.

"Chris!"

"What's wrong," she shouted. Her instinct told her that something was wrong with me, but she had no clue as to what it could have been, or how detrimental it really was. I could hear it in her voice.

"I've been shot," I murmured in a low, listless

voice.

For a second, everything was quiet. So much so that I could not even hear the sound of her breathing through the receiver, and then she screamed.

I wanted to say something to her, anything to try to calm her down, but I was not able to utter a single word. My hand went completely limp, and the phone fell to the pavement.

In the background, as the phone lay there on the ground, I could still hear Chris screaming and calling out my name, "Tony, Tony, Tony...say something," but I couldn't. I wasn't even able to move. Everything around me seemed frozen solid, including my body.

Except for the sound of Chris crying and calling out my name over the phone, there was no one else in the world but me.

I began talking to God.

"Oh, God," I cried. "What have I done, Father, to deserve this? Why, God? Why has this happened to me? What have I done, Father!"

In the next instant, an inescapable feeling of slipping more and more into death's grasp engulfed me; yet, I still had enough awareness to close my eyes and begin praying.

"No, God! Please help me, Father! I haven't done anything! God, I love you so much. If I've done anything to hurt you, please forgive me! I love you so much. If this is my time to die, please take care of my wife and my entire family. Please put your arms around my mother, my brothers, and sisters. Please take care of the little angels at my job, God. I'm sorry for all my wrong."

Then, somehow, I found enough strength to lift my arms and reached for heaven. It was as though I were reaching for God, Himself, and even though I knew, and had now accepted the fact that I was dying; I also knew within my spirit that everything was going to be all right. I knew that God had heard my prayers and that I would soon be in His arms. Then my arms dropped and crashed against the pavement. There was no more strength in my body.

While I lay on the ground in complete silence with my eyes closed, I began thinking about my life, my wife, God, and then I opened my eyes.

My vision was a little blurred at first, but then it started clearing, more, and more, and more, until finally, I saw her

approaching me. She was the most beautiful woman I had ever laid eyes on; more so, than anyone I could have ever imagined.

She was wearing a long, white flowing dress, and her gray and black hair was extremely long. She looked as though she could truly be an Angel.

She stood over me for a few moments, then kneeled down, gently took my head, placed it on her lap, and then began to rub my forehead, while every so gently stroking and caressing the side of my face.

"God," she said in a very soft and extremely gentle voice, "what have they done?"

She continued caressing the side of my face.

"It's going to be all right," she said.

At that point, I thought, "She's going to get her dress all bloody."

Another moment or so passed as I lay on the ground looking up at her, and then I closed my eyes.

Sixteen

" ABSENT FROM THE BODY AND PRESENT WITH THE LORD "

It was like something out of a dream. The atmosphere was warm, incandescent, and tranquil. I was floating through the clouds without a care in the world, it seemed. It was amazing because I felt this sudden, enormous flush of peace envelope my entire body and everything was now okay. I knew at that very moment that nothing could ever hurt me again.

I, then, noticed myself floating toward a huge, white cloud and, as I did, a small opening suddenly appeared through it and I could see a huge, sparkling city. The city was, deluged with vivid colors, unlike any I had never seen, or could even imagine in life. The stones, which were a variety of jewels, were stunningly beautiful and radiant.

Everything seemed so peaceful, with a tranquility matched only by the calm, and silence. I felt completely safe and secure. I saw sparkles of glittering light, dashing through the city. Suddenly, the Holy Spirit whispered in my ear, saying, "Those sparkles of light are archangels that never stop praising God saying, Holy, Holy, Holy... is the one true living God!"

It was indescribable and unlike anything, I had ever known. I was looking at heaven.

Then, suddenly, I stop floating. I wondered what was going on. Why was I no longer approaching this wondrous, magnificently beautiful city?

As I stood still, suspended and motionless in the atmosphere, I suddenly heard people talking, children laughing, and birds chirping. It was so beautiful.

I listened for a moment, and then I heard a huge, extremely powerful, yet gentle voice say, "It's not your time. Go back."

Somehow, I knew that this voice was the voice of God Almighty himself, and I was crushed. Why was He telling me to go back? I couldn't understand it.

"It's so beautiful and peaceful here," I thought.

I cried aloud with unrestrained urgency, "No! I don't wanna' go back! I wanna' stay here! Please let me stay here! I don't wanna go back to the hurt and pain, Father."

"Tony, it's not yet your time," He said. "Your work is not yet finished. Go back!"

Suddenly I found myself drifting backward. "No," I shouted, "please let me stay!" but, at that precise moment, I began hurtling backward. As I did, I kept crying out to God with everything in me, "No! No! Please! No!"

I thought to myself; "This can't be happening. I'm so close."

I was so close that I thought I could reach out and touch Heaven's jeweled walls, and believe me I tried. I began stretching my arms out, grabbing for the clouds. If only I could grab hold to one of them I might be able to pull myself back toward that glorious city, but I couldn't. It was no use. I kept hurtling backwards and there was nothing I could do about it.

Seventeen

" RESURRECTED FROM DEATH "

When I eventually opened my eyes, a doctor was standing over me with a sheet in his hand about to place it over my head, but before he could, God knelt down and blew the breath of life back into my body. It was then I realized I was in the hospital. Machines were everywhere. As I lay there looking around, I noticed a tube running from my throat to one of the machines. I suddenly realized that I was on a life support system. My heart began to break.

After realizing where I was and that something was terribly wrong, I noticed a couple of doctors walk into my room, shaking their heads.

One of them smiled and said, "Man, we lost you. What should have been a two-hour operation turned into a seven and a half-hour operation, instead."

I tried to respond, but couldn't. All I could do was lay there, remembering and thinking of how close I had come, only seconds' earlier, it seemed, to actually being in Heaven, and now I was back on earth.

"Surely," I thought, "there must be something awesome, something beyond my wildest imagination and comprehension that God wants me to do, and I have to do it!"

With tubes in my throat and an IV in my veins, I was more hurt by the fact that I was lying in a hospital than anything else.

"Not me," I thought to myself, "I'm a child of God. I have dedicated my life to the Lord's work through music. There's no way this could've happened to me."

But, it had, even though I had just finished a third song for a new CD project I was working on along with two, awesome, praying brothers, who loved the Lord as much as I did.

There I lay, "another victim" of senseless, gang violence and I could not understand why. I did not even know the boys who shot me. As I thought about it more, I just could not understand why something like this could happen to me. I had never in my life, not even once, held a real gun in my hand. My heart was totally crushed at that point.

As the doctors stood there, I wanted so badly to say something but the words just would not come forth. The tube in my throat kept me from uttering a single word. Thoroughly disgusted and severely discouraged, I just closed my eyes, and fell asleep.

Throughout the night and next day, I kept waking up, but I was slipping in and out of consciousness and I was very weak from the surgery.

During my moments of consciousness, I remember seeing different people in my room, standing over my bed, praying for me. Dr. Sherman A. Gordon, the pastor of my church, and a host of friends from the congregation were visiting and praying for me.

People from my job and anyone who had heard about what had happened to me also came to visit and pray for me. A few of them told me later that they thought I was not going to make it because my entire body was swollen,

and I was barely breathing. Still, though, they were all praying, ensuring me that I was going to be all right. It was so good to see the many wonderful people in my life. I felt truly blessed by their caring. I am so very thankful for every one of them and their outpouring of love, concern, and compassion.

***

Early in the morning on the third day, two of my sisters, Vicky and Charlie Mae, and my oldest brother, Robert Lee, flew in from Mississippi to see how I was doing. Leo flew in from New Jersey to see about me, too. I was told that each of them were crying as they rubbed my forehead and held my hands. When I open my eyes and saw them, I couldn't say a single word to comfort them because the trachea tube was still in my throat.

***

During one of my moments when I was conscious, I remember Charlie Mae, my eldest sister, saying, "Tony, mama wants to fly you home right now. She is so very hurt behind this.

She can't believe that something like this has happened to you. You're a preacher."

Even though I was still unable to talk, I began

praying, asking God to comfort my mother.

***

Early the next morning, a doctor told me that he was going to remove the trachea tube and all of the other wires that were hooked up to me.

When he removed the trachea tube, I immediately began gasping for air. He quickly reattached the tube, and said, "Oh my God! Looks like we'll need to place a permanent trachea in your throat," and then turned and walked out of the room, shaking his head.

I said to myself, "God, you made me whole, and whole I will be in the name of Jesus."

A few moments later, the doctor came back into the room along with another doctor, who looked into my eyes, and then said to the other doctor, "No! I'm sure that he can breathe on his own. Let me take it out."

He looked at me and said, "Mr. Davis, take a deep breath and hold it if you can for a few seconds."

I did as he instructed, and then he slowly and gently removed the tube from my throat, saying, "Breathe out Mr. Davis, through your nostrils."

As I did, I softly said "Jesus." Suddenly, I felt air flowing in and out of my nose. I could finally breath on my own for the first time in what seemed like months.

The first doctor could hardly believe his eyes.

"I don't understand," he said in complete amazement, "I took the tube out, and he couldn't breathe at all!"

"Thank you, Jesus," I thought.

The next doctor said, "Mr. Davis, uh, I'm sorry, but we had to cut your throat to perform an emergency operation because you totally stopped breathing...and you flat-lined on us."

I couldn't believe what I was hearing. Did this guy just say that he had to cut my throat? I could barely speak, but I had to try to ask. "Say what? Cut my throat! What are you talking about?"

"We had to do it to bring you back, Mr. Davis."

"Bring me back. Bring me back from where?"

"We almost lost you. Well, actually, we did lose you. So, we had to cut your throat, but we cut it as far away from your vocal cords as we possibly could. Unfortunately with this type of procedure, most of the time the patient either loses their voice all together, or can barely speak again; so please don't be upset if we have to place a permanent trachea into your throat. We don't know if we have to just yet, but there is a strong possibility that we may have to."

"Don't be upset!" I couldn't believe he was asking me not to be upset about never being able to talk again: not to mention losing the ability to sing. I immediately closed my eyes and began praying again, "God, you made me whole, and whole Father I will be. In the name of Jesus!"

I then opened my eyes, just as the doctor said, "Mr. Davis, say something please."

I responded by calling out as best I could the name of my Lord.

"Jesus," I whispered ever so faintly.

"Your voice sounds great," the doctor said, "but still, take it easy, and try not to talk too much."

The doctor then turned and left the room.

Minutes later, my younger brother Leo walked into my room with tears in his eyes. He moved to the side of my bed, took my hand into his, and tightly held it. "Please tell me who did this to you," he asked.

Barely able to speak, I pleaded with him in a low, thorny whisper, "Let it go, Leo. God is going to take care of this."

After that, he just stood by my bedside, as though he were on guard, protecting me, and holding my hand as I fell

asleep.

***

A few days later, July 4th to be exact, an artery specialist visited me with more bad news, as if I had not already heard enough.

"Mr. Davis," he said, "we did our best to save

your left leg, but at the moment we're not quite satisfied with the way that the plastic artery is sitting in your leg. Unfortunately, we may have to amputate your leg. We have another specialist coming in later to look at the artery once we do more x-rays. So please, try and take it easy until then."

***

Later that night, around midnight, a warm feeling, traveled up and down my leg, awakening me, and, my entire body suddenly felt wonderful. There was absolutely no pain at all. I knew at that very moment that God was healing me because I could feel the presence of His Holy Spirit in and all

around me.

***

Early the next morning, I was awakened again, this time by a tickling sensation at the bottom of my left foot.

I opened my eyes and saw my doctor, standing in the midst of seven other doctors; literally surrounding my bed.

"You jumped when I touched the bottom of your foot," my doctor exclaimed.

"Yes, it tickles," I replied.

When I said that it tickled, all of the doctors

looked at one another, amazed, began talking amongst themselves for a moment, and then turned and faced me.

"Mr. Davis, you are a very lucky man. Years ago, with the type of injury that you sustained, we would have had to amputate your leg immediately. You were shot five times. Three times in your left leg and twice in your right. Each bullet that entered your body came out making ten bullet holes in your body.

It is amazing to us how not one of those five bullets touched a single bone in your body. You are a very lucky man."

"I'm not lucky, doctor," I said, "I'm blessed."

The bewildered doctor looked at me and shook his head.

"This is amazing," one of the other doctors said, "We were preparing to try and reset the artery in your leg or amputate it."

"No, this is a blessing," I reiterated.

After a few more minutes of conferring among themselves, while probing at my feet with all types of medical instruments, the doctors began to leave the room. I could tell by their confused looks that they were dumbfounded by what God had done. By the way, that is just the way God is. He gets a kick out of dumbfounding those who think they know it all, and He does it just to show them that He is God, and that He has all power and can do whatsoever He pleases.

A couple of days later, two deputies from the Los Angeles Sheriff's Department entered my room and asked me to look at some pictures of a few, gang members who were known to hang out in the area where I was shot. As I looked through the photos, the negative emotions of anger, hurt, disgust, sadness, pain, and resentment engulfed me.

Still, as I continued looking through the pictures, I never really thought or believed that I would actually see the person who shot me, and then suddenly, the bitter taste of fear nearly consumed my tongue as I realized that I was staring at the face of someone who looked precisely like the person who shot me.

"I think this is him," I said to one of the deputies, standing patiently by my bed.

{*Note: Be advised that the names mentioned hereafter concerning any gang and its affiliated members have been changed for legal purposes, and are therefore fictional.}

The officer took the picture from me, looked at it for a moment, and then said, "His name is Jeffrey Davis, but his street name is "Baby Suicide". He's seventeen years old and is one of the neighborhood drug leaders in that area."

"A mere seventeen years old," I thought. At that moment, a sadness washed over me as I thought of the numerous occasions, I had gone to juvenile correction centers, ministering to young boys and girls over the past three years. I was trying to encourage them to do the right things in life, to let Jesus into their hearts and minds; to turn away from doing so many wrong things in their young lives; and most of all, to never give up on God because He would never give up on them.

I have tried to encourage our youth to walk by faith and not by sight, and love their neighbors and friends in the same way that they would like to be, loved, and treated. All I wanted to do was make a significant life-changing difference in their lives. This has been, and continues to be, my hope and dream: because these kids are our future.

So, as I sat there looking at the photo, I saw a young, frightened black male who could possibly spend many years in prison for this unconscionable crime he had committed against me. In most cases, he would just learn more ways of committing sin while locked up, and then come out of prison worse than he was before he went in. It's no secret that the prison system, even though designed to supposedly reform those individuals who've broken the law against productive citizens, only breeds hardened criminals who, in most cases, find themselves in a never ending revolving door; constantly in and out jail. Current statistics show that at any given time there are over two million black males locked up throughout this country, who are caught up in a never ending revolving door of recidivism for the rest of their lives.

It is so sad because a great number of young people, both male and female of all races and colors have allowed Satan to use and ultimately ruin their lives. All Satan does is sit back delighting at the destruction that he has caused. The Bible says that

Satan goes to and fro in the earth as a roaring lion, seeking whom he may devour.

The key point to this particular scripture is, "as a roaring lion."

Satan is a fake, a bully, and a coward that relies totally on intimidation to frighten and inflict torture on his victims, just like any other coward. The reality is that Satan has no more power over our lives than we allow him to have.

The Bible teaches us in James 4:7, "Submit yourselves therefore to God. Resist the devil, and he will flee from you."

Do not, any of you, submit yourselves to fear. Stand against the evil one. Satan cannot lead you into sin against your own free will.

Remember, God has created and given each of us free will, which is the right to make our own decisions, whatever they may be, right, or wrong. He did this because He wants us to serve Him out of love.

Yes, my beloved, this proves that we as individuals have great power and authority over our own lives and destiny, and that Satan can only do to us what we allow him to do.

Bullet from the Radiator

Bullet from the Tire

Eighteen

" VENGEANCE IS MINE, SAITH THE LORD "

I got up early that morning to pray and seek the face of God. I was very concerned about doing the right thing, and accusing the right individual of a crime that, in my opinion, was cruel and heinous, to say the least.

"Dear, God," I asked, "please anoint me today, deep down in my spirit, and let me know beyond a shadow of doubt that this boy is one of the boys who shot me. Lord, you know that I don't want to blame this young man for a crime if he did not commit it.

I only want justice to come to those that are responsible for harming me."

***

A few hours later, Chris, and I drove to the police station, and the police drove us to the courthouse, located in downtown Los Angeles.

As I slowly and carefully walked with the use of a cane, limping on my left leg into the courtroom, my heart began to pound, harder, and harder. It wasn't out of fear, though, just an eagerness to know if this was actually the boy who shot me. I was filled with such anxiety that the palms of my hands began to sweat.

I sat down and immediately began to feel hurt,

and an exceeding amount of sadness rushed through my heart as I

waited for the young boy to walk through those courtroom doors.

As I continued sitting there, waiting, anger suddenly began to consume Chris and I. Chris was so angry that she said to me, "No matter who comes through those doors, when I testify, I'm going to say that he did it because if he didn't do it, he knows who did, plus, maybe that will frighten him into saying who did it, if he knows."

I turned to Chris and said, "He might not be the one."

Then, with amazing coincidence, Chris' contact lens broke and she could not see well.

We told the police officer and the prosecutor that Chris needed to get another pair of contacts, but we were not permitted to leave the building because the case was about to begin as soon as Jeffrey Daniels entered the room.

So, Chris decided not to testify because she was unable to see well. Chris then said to me, "Someone needs to pay for the pain and suffering we went through!"

When she said that to me, I felt sad, and did not say another word. But then, I thought, "Someone does need to pay for my pain and suffering." I had decided that whoever walked through that door would be the one held responsible because he was a member of the gang that caused this unholy atrocity upon my life: for no reason at all.

After a few more moments, suspects, chained and shackled like the heartless criminals they were, began entering the courtroom.

There were three other cases ahead of mine, so I had to wait before the judge finally ordered the bailiff to bring in Jeffrey Daniels, the suspect who had shot me.

Looking at him, my heart was enraged even more. I didn't understand it. This young, clean-cut black male looked frightened, and although he was not afraid the night that he shot me, I wondered what could he possibly be afraid of now?

He looked around the courtroom as though he didn't belong there, and the spirit of fear attempting to hide the true evil within him, cloaked his face like the hood of anonymity over the head of a heartless executioner. He scanned the courtroom, hoping to recognize who might be responsible for his presence in court, but he didn't see me or, for that matter, maybe he didn't even recognize me, which only made my simmering anger rise to the boiling point.

Here I sat, another victim of useless gang violence: just another face. I was just another human being without meaning and completely unrecognizable to the perpetrator of evil doings.

As I watched from the back of the courtroom, all of a sudden I realized that this young man wasn't one of my shooters, and then I heard the voice of God speaking within my spirit, saying, "Vengeance is mine, saith the Lord thy God. I will fight your battle.

My word says touch not my anointed, and do my prophets no harm."

Suddenly, I felt nothing but peace within my spirit, and it quickly took the place of the intense anger I had experienced just moments before. I had to tell the truth, and do the right thing.

Then the prosecutor called me to the witness stand. As I approached it, still limping on my cane, the prosecutor opened the small door leading to the witness stand. As I

stepped up, I could not pry my eyes away from the young boy, who sat to the right of the courtroom looking at me with fear written all over his face.

As that fear overtook him, he silently mouthed, "I swear to you, man, I didn't shoot you! I swear I didn't shoot you! I didn't, man!"

Without blinking, I looked straight into his eyes and said, "Who did," but he just kept mouthing, "Man, I swear I didn't shoot you!"

Suddenly, the prosecutor asked me to tell the court what happened on that night.

As I gave my testimony, I still couldn't take my eyes away from the boy because of the hurt I had experienced that terrible and dreadful night. He sat there looking at me while his left leg jumped up and down uncontrollably, and sometimes he closed his eyes, as if he were praying.

When I finished my testimony, the prosecutor asked me to step down from the stand and go out of the courtroom, because they were going to review the young boy's testimony.

***

After I sat in the lobby for quite some time, one of the officers finally came and drove Chris and I back to the police station.

***

On the way home, I thought to myself; "What will ever become of that young man? Will he be released and continue committing crimes, or will he turn his life around? I could only pray that he would decide to do the right thing."

I am still praying for him, to this very day. I am praying that he will open his heart and let Jesus in, just as I did years ago, when I was also traveling down a road of self-destruction.

As for the guys who shot me, I'm not going to let it get me down. Sometime it is hard, though, knowing that they are still walking around free, able to do harm to someone else. Nevertheless, I can rest now, assured in the fact that God is going to take care of them for me, and soon. He told me so, Himself.

***

Now, the boys (D.D.T.) and I are back in the studio, finishing up the CD that God had started.

Only God knows what my future holds, I pray daily that He continues to lead me and keep me in His merciful grace.

In conclusion, I'd like once again to remind each and everyone of you who reads this book that the Bible says in Romans 8:28, and I believe what the Bible says, "And we know that all things work together for the good of them that love God, to them who are called according to his purpose."

It's strange, how such a bad experience can turn into a blessed one.

We never know what tomorrow holds or can bring into our lives. It can be good or bad. It is comforting to know, beyond a shadow of doubt, and regardless to whatever

scheme, plot, plan or evil device that Satan uses against us on our journey to the Father, that as long as we keep Jesus as the head of our lives, He will bring us through everything that the devil can and will throw our way. Not even death can hold God's child down.

One of my favorite moments of meditation came from a wonderful radio host in Atlanta, Georgia named Zilla Mays, who went to heaven on September 19, 1995.

During her final broadcast before her death, she said, "Nothing in life can defeat me. For as long as this knowledge remains, I can suffer whatever is happening. For I know that God will break all the chains: chains that are binding me tight in the darkness and trying to fill me with fear. For there is no night without dawning, and I know that, my morning is near.

I pray that this book encourages someone to never give up on faith, because it is going to be all right, and it is going to be a better day.

Tony singing at the Gospel Music of America
in New Orleans 2002

Tony & Rapper Lewy
"The Get It Together Tour"

Fred & Ketric   The Blount Family

Fred & Keshia wedding December 28, 2002

Chris, Feillipa, Cleo & Family   Rickey, Ayuanna, & Ramona

Bryan   &   Chrisd'yon

Tenesah & Johnathan   Tony & Victor Aguilar Sr.

Cleo, Chris, & Feillipa.

Dolores & Abraham

Isadore & Vera

Otha & Vickey

Carlo Wright

Pamela Thomas

Tony & Aunt Willie B.

President Jimmy Carter & Auntie- Leora Bilbro

Auntie Neoma Davis & Family

Robert Lee & Family

Vickie, Uncle Willie & Vera

Uncle Aron

Leo, Leobrian, Tony

Pastor Curtis Brown
{December 1930 to March 2004}

In loving remembrance of my very dear friend, Pastor Curtis Brown.

I thank God for blessing me to meet such a wonderful, kind hearted man Of God, who did all he could to make people happy. I remember when I release my very first, gospel CD project back in July 1999, Pastor Brown opened his church doors to me to do a concert without even knowing me that well when others would not.

He said to me that he did not know me personally, but he knew my spirit. He was very concerned when he heard about the tragedy that came into my life on July 1, 2003. He told me that he always remembered me in his prayers and he knew that the Lord would bring me through my valley experience.

Now, he has gone to the place I never wanted to leave.

God Bless You My Dear Friend
Until we meet again
Tony Davis

Reverend Sherman A. Gordon, D. Minister

Since the Biblical days of old, God has been using great men of faith who believed in what appeared to be impossible because they trusted in the God of invincibility. Men, like Abraham who moved according to the will of God and went out not fully aware of where he was going, nor aware of all that was in store for him.

David, he went out against Goliath even when the crowd was saying, "David, you can't conquer Goliath, He's too big"! However, David moved in the faith that the God he served was BIGGER.

Paul faced death numerous times, but never feared. Such is the testimony of Tony Davis. Staring death in the face, he embraced himself in the comforting words of His Maker who declared "It's Not Yet Your Time". Having cheated death and now laughing in its face, Tony can boldly remark, "Heaven is Real", and God is Good."

Sherman A. Gordon, D. Minister
"NEW PHILADELPHIA A.M.E. CHURCH"

Pastor Vicki Lee

Minister Tony,

From the day, God had our paths to cross, what a divine purpose & plan. My life and ministry has been so inspired and super blessed to have you as part of our team at Saints of Value Ministries. Only to see how He (God) has used you in such a Supernatural way. Blessing millions as you preach the word of God, may it be by WORD and SONG. God has truly blessed you, Tony. Carry His Word! I want to encourage you with a key to the work of the ministry… OBEY GOD! Walk out by faith, and Trust him. In that, you will always win.

Your Friend, sister and co-Laborer in the gospel.

"SAINTS OF VALUE MINISTERIAL TRAINING CENTER"

Assistant Pastor Charles A. Johnson

There is a special bond between Tony and myself. Certainly, we as born again Believers and fellow ministers, are tied together, and, in the natural as co-workers at Willing Workers, Inc., we are bound.

However, there is something else, which binds us together in a profound way. We both have experience the miracle of God's healing power. Tony's testimony is well documented within the pages of this book, and while my personal testimony might not be quite as spectacular as his, I can still proclaim the awesome healing power of God. I was diagnosed with prostate cancer and surgery was scheduled for January 12, 1999. I read in the 5th Chapter of James that if one calls for the elders of the church to anoint him with oil and pray the prayer of faith, he would be healed. I obeyed that word and began to confess and claim my healing.

Sometimes I testify to the walls of the miracle healing God bestowed upon me. I join in with my brother Tony in praising God from whom all blessings flow.

Carl A. Johnson
Assistant Pastor,
"ABIDING LOVE CHRISTIAN FELLOWSHIP CHURCH"

Pastor Henry A. Johnson

Minister Tony Davis, your testimony has been a blessing me, and the New Dawn Missionary Baptist Church of Pasadena. The beloved apostle John said in the book of Revelation, Rev. 22:8, "I, John, am the one who heard and saw these things".

What did John see? He said in Revelation 22:1, "he showed me the river of living water, sparkling like crystal, flowing from the throne of God and of the Lamb down the middle of the broad street of the city. On both sides of the river was the tree of life bearing 12 kinds of fruit, producing its fruit every month. The leaves of the tree are for healing the nations and there will no longer be any curse".

Therefore, Tony continue to tell your story of what you have seen and heard in Heaven, and our God will bless you for your faithfulness.

Your friend and brother in the Lord,

Pastor Henry A. Johnson, Pastor/Teacher
New Dawn Missionary Baptist Church

Apostle Robbie Horton, PhD.

Tony Davis, known as evangelist, gospel artist, and entrepreneur to many, but he really is an end-time product of God's supernatural power and grace. He is a messenger that has witnessed the Love of God, and God's eternal plan for our life. He is a witness for Christ that has an impact upon everything that he does for God.

I know that this book will have an attended effect of the anointing upon your life. I count it as a great honor in knowing him as a vessel and a servant for Christ as well as one of my spiritual sons.

Apostle Robbie Horton PhD.
"ANOINTED CONNECTION INTERNATIONAL MINISTRIES"

Dr. Larry C. Jackson

For almost thirty years as Pastor of Gethsemane Christian Love Baptist Church, upon approaching the pulpit, I often proclaimed what the bible says in Deuteronomy Chapter 28, Verse 14, which reads: "I am the head and not the tail, I am above only and not beneath", therefore no matter what may come my way, I am above my situation, Jesus made it so, I have the victory".

When I heard what had happened to my dear friend, I knew without a shadow of a doubt that the same God that raised Lazarus from the dead would raise Tony out of his tragedy. Now, look and see what the Lord has done. I know that this book is going to touch, move, and inspire thousands of lives!

God Bless You My Friend!

Pastor Larry C. Jackson
{ GETHSEMANE CHRISTIAN LOVE BAPTIST CHURCH }

Pastor Charles Mackie

Same God, Different Situation

The same God that tested Israel in Deuteronomy chapter 8, to see what was in their hearts and if they would keep His commandments and remember Him as he moved them in another level of abundant prosperity is the same God that is at work today.

God made a promise to your forefathers of blessings that they might have missed by not seeking and trusting in the Lord, or it could have been sheer disobedience to His word. The good new is, however, is that His word will not return to Him void. His word of blessings went forth and is available to you if you would just trust and obey His word.

God wants to bless you more than you can ask or think. Trust Him today, for God is the same, yesterday, today, and forever.

Pastor Charles Mackie
"KEEPING IT REAL" LIGHT HOUSE

Dr. Paula D. Johnson

Dr. Paula D. Johnson

My Son Tony,

Truly it was God's doing, and marvelous in his sight, and God get all the glory for the things he has done in your life, Especially your outstanding achievement with this great book!

Love Always!

Dr. Paula D. Johnson
(Your Spiritual Mother)
"FAITH AND LOVE OUTREACH MINISTRY"

**Rick Mizuno
(Author)**

I truly admire Brother Tony Davis on many levels. He is a man with a good heart towards others, but even more, he has a heart for God. He is an honorable man, but even more that, he honors his wife before men. Needless to say, Brother Tony has a tremendous will to live, to live a life that is pleasing to our Lord and Savior Jesus Christ. His miraculous story is so remarkable it seems almost fictional but in fact… it is all true.

Rick Mizuno, motivational speaker, founder of THINK RIGHT Concepts and author of the new provocative romance novel, ***"50/50 Split."***

For more info visit: **www.5050split.net**
email: love@5050split.net

Ron Lowe

To God be the Glory! Great things He has done! God is still working miracles in the lives of His people. Tony Davis is a living testimony of God's blessings. His testimony affirms the lyrics of a popular gospel song, "God has not promised me sunshine; but a little rain mixed with God's sunshine; a little pain, so that you can appreciate the good times".

Truly, Tony has seen his share of sunny days, as well as the dark, sable, and cloudy days. Yet, his faith in God remains steadfast. This book chronicles the miraculous story of Tony Davis.

Congratulations, Tony on the publication of your book. May it be a blessing to everyone who reads it.

Isaiah 40:31 – But they that wait upon the Lord shall renew their strength; they shall mount up with wings as eagles; they shall run and not be weary; and they shall walk and not faint.

Ron Brown

Tony Davis is a gifted and anointed man of God. His testimony will inspire and encourage many to seek an intimate relationship with Jesus Christ because Tony is a walking testimony to God's awesome power. His book and music will reflect that and have a powerful impact on all those who experience this richly blessed ministry.

JOAN ADRIENNE STURGIS

During the time I spent editing this incredibly inspiring biography,
I was given a firsthand lesson about the awesome power of God, and how He allows the human spirit to triumph over unprovoked and unspeakable ordeals in our lives.

It is not "by accident" or a "stroke of luck," that Tony Davis's life was spared on the night he stared into the eyes of a cold-blooded executioner. It was through God's love and grace that Tony was given a second chance. With that chance, Tony shares his remarkable story that enlightens and inspires us in our walk with God, and the importance of learning to forgive.

Joan-Adrienne Sturgis
Editor

Avan C. Hardwell Sr.

First, I thank Almighty God for assigning me into Tony*s heart when he decided to write about his life. I am honored that he asked me to write this book for him. While doing so, I was taken down life's memory lane on several occasions. So much so, until I came to realize that our lives paralleled in many, many ways and I actually felt as though I was writing about my own life's experiences on many occasions. I had to remind my self several times that this book is not about me, but someone else.

I am also a musician. I have learned through the years that when the hand of God is upon your life, and He has chosen you to do a work for Him, it doesn't matter how talented you are, your status in life, or whom you may know, until you fall into the will of God and walk His narrow, path of righteousness, your life will never be what you desire it to be.

Brothers* and Sisters*, God is truly an awesome, gracious and forgiving God who specializes in doing the impossible. It is my greatest hope and desire that something written in this book of truth and spiritual inspiration will change the lives of all who may read it, and that those lives will never be the same again.

God bless you all

Avan C. Hardwell
Guitarist, Vocalist, Composer, Entrepreneur
Author (Heaven Is Real)

Made in the USA
Charleston, SC
24 February 2013